PRAISE FOR *KNITTING* ͡

"This debut gives tender and keen insight into the experience to the US and the challenges a preteen faces integrating into the 'Promised Land.'
—ANA CASTILLO,
author of *Black Dove: Mamá, Mi'jo, and Me*

"Claudia D. Hernández's exquisite new memoir is a breathtaking read. She is a beautiful storyteller, whose raw honesty sings on the page with a kind of fiery joy and longing of what it means to be a family."
—KERRY MADDEN,
author of the Appalachian Maggie Valley Trilogy

"La Diablita, the tomboy, wrote these searingly honest, la verdad, stories of crossing to *the other side* from her beloved Guatemala to her now home, the USA. Poesía is also sprinkled throughout, her prayers. *Listen*, you'll believe every word as La Diablita knits the fog beyond man-made borders. The fog is love."
—ALMA LUZ VILLANUEVA,
author of *Song of the Golden Scorpion*

"An extraordinary hybrid collection of stunning poetry and even more awe-inspiring prose, evoking the universal journey of identity that we all go through as people, immigrants, and artists."
—ADRIAN ERNESTO CEPEDA,
author of *Flashes & Verses . . . Becoming Attractions*

"This debut is so much more than an immigrant's story. It is an ode to the resilience of the human spirit. A hymn to the power of poems and stories as agents of personal liberation and social change. In any language. Any culture. Anywhere in the world. ¡Brava, Claudia!"
—LUCHA CORPI,
author of *Confessions of a Book Burner:*
Personal Essays and Stories

"Part torch song and part excavation, this is a coming-of-age story about a young girl from Guatemala crossing the border and making a life that is *hers* in America. It is also a book of our times, a story of struggle and resilience, a warrior song that refuses to look or run away."
—MELISSA R. SIPIN,
editor in chief, *TAYO Literary Magazine*

Sovereignty by Claudia D. Hernández

KNITTING THE FOG

Claudia D. Hernández

FEMINIST PRESS
AT THE CITY UNIVERSITY
OF NEW YORK
NEW YORK CITY

325
HER

Published in 2019 by the Feminist Press
at the City University of New York
The Graduate Center
365 Fifth Avenue, Suite 5406
New York, NY 10016

feministpress.org

First Feminist Press edition 2019

  This book was made possible thanks to a grant from New York State Council on the Arts with the support of Governor Andrew M. Cuomo and the New York State Legislature.

 This book is supported in part by an award from the National Endowment for the Arts.

 This book is supported in part by an award from the Shelley & Donald Rubin Foundation.

The author would like to thank José Hernández Díaz for his English translations of "Mayuelas's Mill," "Tejiendo la niebla," "Ardor de cuerpo," and "Kim Ayu—Vení Pa' Ca."

First printing July 2019

Cover design by Suki Boynton
Cover photograph by Claudia D. Hernández
Text design by Drew Stevens

Library of Congress Cataloging-in-Publication Data

Names: Hernández, Claudia D., author.
Title: Knitting the fog / Claudia D. Hernández.
Description: [New York City : Feminist Press, 2019]
Identifiers: LCCN 2018049649 (print) | LCCN 2018059181 (ebook) | ISBN
    9781936932559 (Ebook) | ISBN 9781936932542 (pbk.)
Subjects: LCSH: Hernández, Claudia D. | Women authors, American--21st
    century--Biography. | Guatemalan American authors--Biography.
Classification: LCC PS3608.E76595 (ebook) | LCC PS3608.E76595 Z46 2019
    (print) | DDC 813/.6--dc23
LC record available at https://lccn.loc.gov/2018049649

AUG 2 2 2019

Para mi mamá y mis hermanas.
And to those who continue
to cross to the other side,
leaving their loved ones behind.

CONTENTS

PART IV: RETURNING TO MY MOTHERLAND

PART I

LIFE IN PARADISE,
ALSO KNOWN AS HELL

Facts on How to Be Born: Life

This is what the partera told my mother the day I was born:
Boys are usually born facing down and girls are born facing up.

Not you, Mamá scolded me. *You came out of me, facing up, a girl.*
But midway out, you spun your body around like the head of a barn

owl. Ghostly, pale. *There were times you acted like a girl, other*
times like a varón.   *Like a tomboy*, I assured her.

Tía Soila buried my umbilical cord next to the tallest tamarindo
tree. I always wondered which one, they were all tall. Unlike

my sisters and I, distinct in size, shape, and temperamento. No
one questioned it; we assumed it had to do with our ancestors'

genes. Two months later, after my birth, Mamá registered me
under Claudia Denise Hernández Ramos at the civil registry of

Guatemala. The secretary typed Penise instead of Denise. I grew
up pretending I was never given a middle name. At the age of

nineteen, I returned to Guatemala, alone, to change the P to a D.
I never questioned why Mamá never did. On that trip, I discovered

my last name should have been Rossi instead of Hernández. *O mother.*
I love you dearly.   That's all I was able to say to her over the phone.

Tempting Mud

Mamá was always running away from something, someone. Her present, her past, the hunger that chased her, Papá's drunkenness and obsessiveness, her mother's abandonment, the heat of Mayuelas or the coldness of Tactic, her beauty— her long hair.

I remember when Mamá would bathe Consuelo and me together in the pila, a washbasin made out of cement. I was four and Consuelo was six. We didn't have hot water; our pila was out in the patio surrounded by the shade of the tamarindo trees. The water came straight from the river, cold and fresh. Mamá never allowed us to drink it.

"It's stale! You'll grow a solitaria, a tapeworm, in your tummy," she would say.

The washbasin was filled with water. It had one sink on each side. One sink had a ribbed surface and it was usually used for hand-washing laundry. The other sink was for doing dishes. Its surface was smooth. Mamá would sit both Consuelo and me on the ribbed sink so that we wouldn't slip. The pila was high off the ground.

"Sindyyyy!" Mamá would yell. "Help me rinse the girls."

Sindy was my oldest sister—eight years older than me. She acted like my second mother whenever she babysat me and later on when Mamá left. There were times I hated Sindy for that.

Mamá's fingernails were always long and sharp. She scrubbed my head furiously with the cola de caballo shampoo. The Mane 'n Tail always burned my eyes. We hadn't heard of baby shampoo in those days. Sindy's job was to pour buckets of water over me. I felt like I was drowning every time the water hit the crown of my head. I somehow managed to breathe through my mouth as the see-through, soapy veil of water covered my face.

After the bath, Mamá would dress us up in summer dresses to keep us fresh in the scalding heat of Mayuelas, where the ceiba trees and mango trees bloomed with tenacity. Mamá kept us clean. She fed us three times every day: huevitos tibios, soft-boiled eggs, and sweet bread with a cup of milk or a Coca-Cola. Sometimes she fed us Nestlé Cerelac by itself—completely dry. It was my favorite.

I remember Mamá was always moody. I never knew why.

"You two better not get dirty!" she'd yell after bathing us.

I loved playing outside in the mud.

One summer day, the mud felt especially cold and refreshing on my skin. Nobody was around to keep an eye on me. Sindy and Consuelo were inside the house with Mamá doing chores. I decided to taste the mud.

I grew up listening to stories about how four-year-old Sindy loved to eat clumps of dirt from Tía Soila's adobe kitchen walls. I was four, and I wanted to see for myself why Sindy loved it so much. Tía Soila was Mamá's aunt, but we also called her Tía.

I knew exactly what I was doing, and I knew it was wrong. Sindy got beat up many times for eating dirt. I looked around one more time before picking up a handful of mud. I was nervous. I was terrified of Mamá.

I hid my dirty hands behind my back, and before I knew it, I found myself grinding rocks with my baby teeth. Two seconds later, I spat everything out and ran to the outhouse. No one saw me. I couldn't get rid of the salty-chalky taste in my mouth.

I spat and spat everywhere, in the darkness of the toilet, all over the dirt floor until my mouth felt dry. Eventually, I began to appreciate the petrichor scent trapped in my mouth. I finally understood why Sindy desired clumps of dirt in her mouth. It was a different type of hunger we both had.

nothing ever hurt: fragmented memory

By the time I was five, I became numb to seeing Papá passed out
in the cantina,
                    drunk and penniless; his pockets inside out,
                    lying on the street
             naked, while Guatemala's army baptized the
             Chuchumatán Mountains
with rifles,   machetes.

At home, Mamá became a see-through cup ready to explode
from the deepest red of her chest. There were times she
wished Ríos Montt's regime would take him away. But
instead, she broke things   with her wings.
             Empty plumes impregnated the air.

It was usually Tía Soila who broke up their fights.
             Mamá would gather the three of us under her arms.
             Her collar—
adorned with purple pearls, while Papá's eye—bleeding with
whiskey—was
scarred by her tacón.

             Far away, the mountains moaned
                          with the Ixil people's burning trees—
                          screeching bones.

I don't mean to tell you how my sister Consuelo cried,
             latching to Mamá's thigh, begging her not to look for
             him and fight him

like a mad Quetzal. Consuelo grew emotionally thick skin
                    wings.

I don't mean to tell you how my sister Sindy, at the age of
nine,
                    became my second mother. Soon, she developed a
                    special gaze, the one
where one eye can see right through you, while the other one
                              lingers for imaginary horizons to
                              perch on.

What I do mean to tell you is how I felt ecstatic running from
house to house,
                    seeking shelter, hiding from Papá's fluttering
                    wrath. I distracted
myself playing by the riverbank, creating dolls of mud and
clay—bloodstained—
                    from the mouth of the Río Negro/río ardiente—
                                        I pretended to be god.

I never asked why we always went back. I laughed out loud
and spun around,
                    blurring everyone's faces until I'd fall on the ground
                    skinning
my fragmented memory; nothing ever hurt. Now at thirty-
four, I pick Mamá's

broken feathers,   from my throat;   while eighty-six-year-
old Ríos Montt
spreads his wings in the comfort of his golden home;

                    unexpected overturned   veredicto.

Crying—See/Saw—Laughing

Everyone in town was afraid of Mamá; she had a permanent frown on her forehead. No one dared to mess with her. She carried herself in such a way, insinuating that she was good at everything, including cutting her own hair, my sisters' hair, and mine.

She always kept her hair shoulder length, wavy, 1920s flapper style until she began to eat it at an older age. She began to pluck each strand, one by one, and cry quietly in the darkness of her bedroom. Consuelo and I modeled short bob hairstyles, looking more like older women than six- and four-year-old girls. Sindy had long hair. If Mamá ever cut Sindy's hair, it wasn't noticeable because of her large, bouncy curls.

Mamá had a monthly hair-cutting routine. When our bangs grew too long and started getting in our eyes, she trimmed our bobs with her twelve-inch, heavy-duty scissors—the same ones she used to cut the fabric for our homemade dresses, and the husks from corn.

She was in a bad mood the day she decided to cut Consuelo's hair. She yanked at Consuelo's hair even though it was untangled—straighter than pine needles. Consuelo didn't complain. We both knew that Papá had not come home the night before. We knew he had fallen asleep at Miriam's bar, like the "typical drunk he was."

Mamá didn't simply trim Consuelo's hair, she chopped away at it while Consuelo sat there silently taking it all in. Sindy was at school. I hid behind the curtains and, through the window, noticed Papá returning home, walking toward the door.

My legs trembled watching him approach the door,

stumbling around, his head drooping over, his body tilting to the left. I began to sway back and forth, just like him, realizing that I had to pee. I was terrified, but oddly excited to know that something bad was about to happen. I peed a little on myself. Letting it out felt good.

Papá didn't have his keys. Both his pants' front pockets were sticking out like deflated off-white balloons. The dancers at Miriam's bar—or the putas, as Mamá referred to them—would usually send him home two days later after they had drank all his monthly check.

Papá knocked twice on the door, but Mamá continued with her chopping, ignoring him. I peed a little bit more on myself. He banged on the door louder, harder. Consuelo began to sob quietly and I continued to hide behind the curtains. My puddle of piss kept growing.

We should have been used to watching them fight like professional wrestlers in front of us. Sometimes Consuelo served as their referee, getting in between them, absorbing some of the punches and scratches. If we were living in Mayuelas, Tía Soila would intervene. If we were living in Tactic, Mamatoya, my grandma, would separate them with her broom or her machete.

I was afraid of Papá. I hated seeing blood drawn from any part of Mamá's body. I didn't mind so much when Mamá would scratch Papá's face with her sharp nails, or use the pointy heel of her shoe as a hammer to attempt to hit him in the eye, like a nail. I secretly cheered for her. I was aware of Papá's height and strength. He was twice her size.

Papá didn't need anyone cheering for him. Most of the time those cheers were more like cries and wails. Consuelo would always find a way to get involved in their brawl: Pulling on Papá's arm. Tugging on his leg. Begging. Praying. But no one would listen. Sindy would usually cry quietly, too. Her body would shrink while sitting on a chair, or hiding behind a door. She was too thin and fragile to get involved. I usually hid behind something or someone's skirt.

Five minutes later, Consuelo was free to roam the house with an itchy back and a red naked neck. She cried when Papá broke down the living room door, but I continued to laugh, nervously, nonstop, behind the curtain.

After every one of their fights, I became rowdier, with an unstoppable, energetic personality. Consuelo became emotionally strong and observant. Sindy became a quiet, angry, depressed adolescent. Mamá couldn't find a lasting solution to get rid of Papá. She suffered. We suffered. Even Papá suffered because he didn't know how to stay sober. He didn't know how to love Mamá and us the way we deserved to be loved.

Consuelo and I always knew what to do when people and things got broken around the house. That afternoon, we decided to run to the backyard and climb on the muddy wooden seesaw that sat balancing on three maroon bricks piled on top of each other. We were not in the mood for another show.

Even though Consuelo was two years older than me, we were almost the same weight. Somehow, with my tomboyish ways, I managed to weigh down the seesaw by pushing harder. I wanted to send Consuelo soaring into the air to help her forget the commotion inside of the house. But I couldn't even get her to smile her Mona Lisa smile. I, on the other hand, continued to laugh harder. I wasn't sure whether I was laughing at the tingling flies I felt inside my stomach while coming down on the seesaw, or at Consuelo's new hairstyle.

Consuelo continued to sob as she went up and down. And I couldn't control my laughter. No one noticed that my underwear was still wet.

Becoming Papel Picado

I have no one to mourn on the day of the dead.
No one close to me has passed, unnoticed—

All three of my so-called papás walk with screeching
Bones, lost calacas mourning my mother, while

She dances alone, wrapped in her traje dorado,
Transparente. She no longer braids her hair;

She eats it every night, in the dark. She likes to
Pretend that no one can hear her aullidos

When she plucks each strand, one by one.
I have never erected an altar, not even for

Tío Edwin, my mother's brother, Que en Paz
Descanse. He passed when I was eighteen-

Years-old; he was only thirty-three. I was far from
Home. The Family still questions and blames:

Why him and not me? Why him and not you!
He had a promising life.

I have never painted my face on the day of the
Dead. But every year, I devour el pan de muerto;

I drown it in my café. I don't like to dance with
Calaveras either, I prefer to visit and photograph

A stranger's tombstone in South America, where
I find myself mourning my mother's duende,

Even though she continues to cut me like purple
Papel picado with her backbone-machete.

Pollita trasquilada

I remember the day Consuelo returned home from school crying. It was the day after her seventh birthday. She couldn't hide her face behind her hair; it was too short. She didn't even bother to say hi to Mamá. She went straight to our bedroom, sank her face in the pillow, and left Tía Soila and me behind.

Mamá sat on her cot and didn't bother to ask Consuelo what the problem was. Consuelo kept everything to herself, just like Mamá did. She cried quietly, alone in the corner of her bed. When I entered the bedroom, I sat next to her, and began caressing her choppy new hairdo. Mamá waited patiently for Tía Soila to come. I could hear the grinding of Mamá's dentures from across the room while Tía Soila avoided Mamá's wandering eye.

Earlier that morning when she dropped off Consuelo at school, Tía Soila witnessed how Eufemia and Jaquelyn made fun of her new hairstyle. Tía Soila saw both mother and daughter laugh and point fingers at Consuelo like two preschoolers. Consuelo ignored them like a mature young woman even though she was only a second grader.

Tía Soila didn't actually hear when Eufemia called Consuelo a "pollita trasquilada," a little chick with sheared feathers. She was too far away from Consuelo's classroom door, but she did notice Eufemia making gestures with her hands, mocking Consuelo's hair. Most people from Mayuelas are crude and lack common sense. The raw heat melts their brain night and day, that's what Mamá always said.

I once overheard Tía Soila say that Eufemia and Mamá had been really good friends when they were young, but their friendship had soured with age. No one really knows what happened between them; some family members believe that Eufemia had a thing for Papá. Mamá never shared her problems with anyone except Tía Soila. And Tía Soila never told Mamá's secrets, ever.

I never liked Eufemia. She was known in Mayuelas as an arrogant, good-looking whore. Mamá never allowed us to play with her daughter, Jaquelyn, even though she and Consuelo had been classmates since kindergarten. I didn't like Jaquelyn either because she was a stuck-up girl with her beautiful, long, chocolate curls. I couldn't help feeling envious of her hair.

As soon as Tía Soila sat on her cot, Mamá questioned her, but she couldn't get anything out of her. Consuelo continued sobbing quietly on her bed. I could sense Mamá's anger. When something wasn't right, her face would swell up and burn purple. Her cleverness was sharper than her knives. Tía Soila knew Mamá's rage even better than her own. She knew it was best to stay quiet. She tried.

While Consuelo lay on her bed, I sat next to her, pretending to caress her hair. I wanted to listen to Mamá and Tía Soila's conversation. I always pretended not to know anything or understand what the adults were saying.

"I think she's not happy with her new hairstyle, that's all," said Tía Soila, avoiding Mamá's glare.

"Tell me the truth, Tía Soila! Look me in the eye and tell it to me like it is!" Mamá snapped.

"I'm not sure what happened this morning, but I think la Eufemia and la Jaquelyn made fun of her," Tía Soila finally admitted. I wanted to pull both their hair. Who were they to make fun of my sister?

Sure enough, Mamá's face swelled up and turned purple. She walked out of the room practically expelling flames. I ran after her. I knew she was headed to Eufemia's restaurant on Mayuelas's main route, where all the guaguas from la capital or from Zacapa zoomed by.

I had witnessed Mamá defend herself from Papá like a vicious beast. I wasn't sure what she was capable of doing to another woman for mocking her young. I felt shivers of anxiety crawl up my spine. I felt like peeing on myself again, but this time I held it in. I wanted to stop Mamá from confronting Eufemia, but I didn't know how. I thought of fainting the way I always did every time I was spanked or had my feelings hurt by an adult.

At a young age, maybe when I was two or three, I learned to suffocate myself with my own cries. The lack of air reaching my lungs would cause me to faint momentarily. I had already used that trick too many times to avoid a spanking. But I couldn't. I couldn't even fake it.

"Go back to the house, Claudia!" Mamá yelled at me.

I continued to follow her from a distance, pretending to be a detective trying to solve a mystery without bloodshed. She was possessed and determined to put Eufemia in her place. I couldn't throw myself on the floor and pretend to faint. She would have left me there, lying on the road. Mamá knew me too well.

In the middle of the road, she bumped into cousin Celia, who had the biggest mouth in Mayuelas.

"Victoria!" she called.

Mamá ignored her and continued stomping her feet, leaving animal tracks on the dusty path. Celia ran behind her, caught up to her, and said, "I heard that whore Eufemia called Consuelo a pollita trasquilada."

Mamá stopped cold in the middle of the road, didn't say a word to Celia, and simply took a few steps back to grab my hand, yanking me from behind a dry, naked bush. She was aware of her surroundings at all times.

We began walking together toward Mayuelas's main road, where all the guaguas and cars passed by at a hundred miles an hour, leaving the village behind. People avoided crossing this route because so many had been run over.

Mamá held my hand tight as she stopped to look both ways. She knew my little legs wouldn't keep up with hers. So she picked me up and galloped across the road like a burnt gazelle. Cousin Celia ran behind us. She was nosy. She knew what Mamá was capable of doing and she didn't want to miss it. Nothing interesting ever happened in Mayuelas, except when someone got shot, had an affair, left for El Norte, or got run over by a car.

Eufemia's restaurant was a little shack with an outside patio facing the road and was, for the most part, always empty. Mamá put me down as we got closer. Eufemia was behind the counter. She only had two customers, who were both sitting on high stools, drinking beers. She placed two cold Gallos before them and stepped outside, wiping her hands on her blue apron.

There was a ditch adjacent to the restaurant. Mamá left me on the other side of it with cousin Celia. Before crossing the ditch, she got on her knees and said to me, "Don't move, you understand, sompopo?" Sompopo, a red ant, was one of the many nicknames Mamá had for me. Abispa, a wasp, was my favorite one because, according to Mamá, I stung people with my insatiable energy and charisma.

I nodded. My heart began to beat like a drum being struck by a baseball bat.

Facing Eufemia, Mamá barked an insult like a Rottweiler, "Hija'la gran puta! What did you call my daughter today?"

Eufemia shamelessly laughed and responded, "Pollita trasqui—"

Mamá didn't allow her to finish her sentence and grabbed her by the hair with both hands. She dragged her to the ditch next to me. They fell in there, right before my eyes. I began to cry. I was used to seeing Papá and Mamá try and poke each other's eyes out, but I had never seen Mamá rolling in a ditch with another woman. They looked like pigs waddling in the mud—hungry and thirsty for war.

Cousin Celia held me, shouting, "Dale, Victoria! Teach that whore a lesson." More people began to gather, watching both women roll on the ground like circus animals, entertaining the crowd.

Mamá was a wild animal. She was on top of Eufemia, scratching her face, ripping at her clothes. Eufemia protected her face in vain. It was gushing with blood. When I saw the blood, I didn't know where it was coming from. I wanted to faint, but I didn't want to leave Mamá alone. She didn't need my help, but I knew she was in trouble when the police got there.

Mamá All to Myself

Three policemen dressed in army fatigues arrived and pulled Mamá off of Eufemia. Eufemia sat on the muddy ground crying, holding her face, and unsuccessfully trying to attach her skin back in place.

One of the policemen picked Eufemia off the ground. When she saw Mamá being handcuffed, she ran up to Mamá and punched her in the face like a coward. Mamá's nose began to bleed. No sounds came out of her mouth. I yelled. I wanted to kick Eufemia's crooked shins, but one of the policemen grabbed her and handcuffed her immediately.

I ran up to Mamá and latched on to her thigh like a starving tick. I cried hysterically. A policeman tried to detach me from her leg, but Mamá yelled at him, "You better not touch my daughter. You know well who I am!"

He let me be and allowed me to stay with Mamá. I rode in the back of a beat-up truck with both Mamá and Eufemia. A policeman sat in between them. I sat on Mamá's lap. The warm wind caressed my face and disheveled my hair. The sun was almost setting. The sky seemed to explode with pinkish-orange dismay. I sensed that something terrible was going to happen.

The evening tasted like burnt trash. Sitting on Mamá's lap, I wondered if Tía Soila was incinerating her trash at exactly that moment, the way she did every evening as the sun sunk in the horizon. The truck's siren was weak. It broke down on the way to the police station in Gualán, another town half an hour away from Mayuelas.

When we arrived at the station, General Martínez greeted

Mamá courteously. No one paid attention to Eufemia even though she was a beautiful woman. I guessed people already knew of her reputation back in Mayuelas. She kept crying as blood continued to flow down her face.

Eufemia didn't have a husband to bail her out, and Papá was out of town. I sat there admiring how Mamá argued with the general.

"If I have to spend a night in jail, Eufemia better stay as well. This is between her and me. The problem has been solved."

"You're both spending the night here," said one of the guards as he walked Mamá and Eufemia to an empty cell with no windows. I quickly ran to Mamá and clung to her leg, screaming and wailing. I wanted to be with Mamá, especially since she was going to share the same cell with Eufemia. I couldn't leave her in there alone with that woman.

"Let Claudia spend the night with me, Anibal!" pleaded Mamá to General Martínez. With his pointer finger, he ordered the guards to let me in. The cell was bare, with only a cold cement floor. There were no beds or chairs to sit on, and no bathroom, only a bacinilla, a plastic bedpan, placed in the corner of the cell.

"It smells like death in here," Mamá said.

"It smells like mud and bish," I said, recognizing the residue of urine left behind in the bedpan by other inmates. I knew too well bish's unique odor because it smelled like cooked corn. I had experienced several of those accidents in my five years of life. We sat there for hours. It was too late to have visitors. Tía Soila and my sisters would have to wait until the morning to see us.

"How long are we going to stay here, Mamá?" I asked.

"Only tonight, sompopito. Your dad and Tía Soila will be here tomorrow morning."

"What about Sindy and Consuelo?" I asked, pretending to be concerned about them.

"Don't worry, they'll be fine with Tía Soila," she assured me. Mamá and I embraced each other in one corner while Eufemia sat in the other, weeping alone.

When it finally got dark, General Martínez gave us pieces of cardboard to place on the cement. I lay in the dark next to Mamá. She didn't talk much, but instead snuggled me and caressed my head. I had Mamá all to myself. I fell asleep. It seemed like Eufemia had a fever and kept having nightmares throughout the night. Her whimpers woke me up several times.

"Go back to sleep," Mamá whispered in my ear.

Time went by fast when Mamá held me close. Her sharp nails massaged my scalp until it became numb. Mamá's embrace felt like paradise.

The next day, Tía Soila and Papá came to pick us up. There was no one there for Eufemia. The guards let her go and she walked home alone.

I was only five years old when I spent my first night in jail. On that night, Mamá was mine, only mine.

Northbound

Mamá didn't have the courage to wake me up at five in the morning the day she left illegally for the United States. Tía Soila saw her sitting in the dark, caressing my face and whispering in my ear how much she loved me. Even though I was asleep, trapped in a dream, I remember hearing her distant voice: "I adore you, my sompopito!" Why didn't I force my eyes open? When I woke up, Mamá was gone.

"Why didn't you wake me, Tía Soila?" I cried.

"Claudita, your mother told me not to; she thought it would be best. She was afraid that if you saw her leave, she wouldn't find the strength to look you in the eye and still go."

I couldn't believe Mamá was gone, just like that. I was seven and I felt an emptiness gnawing at my insides. The house didn't look the same. It was missing her lavender smell.

Both my older sisters were still crying even though they got to say goodbye to her. At least they got to walk her to the bus station and hug her one last time.

Why didn't they wake me up? I could have smelled her face again.

"She'll be back for us, Claudita," Consuelo said, trying to comfort me. But even she couldn't hold her tears back. Consuelo was only nine years old, but sometimes she acted like she was older than Sindy.

Sindy was fifteen when Mamá left pa' El Norte. I didn't get to see much of Sindy's face after she came back from the bus station. She hid on the corner bed in the room we all shared, and skipped her meals.

"I hope she doesn't get sick," Tía Soila said, looking at Consuelo and me.

"She'll get hungry, eventually," Consuelo responded.

I was already hungry. My hunger grew more every day after Mamá left.

Tía Soila's eyes were red and swollen, but she didn't cry in front of us. She loved Mamá like a daughter. Tía Soila had taken care of Mamá since she was six years old.

Mamá had asked Tía Soila to care for us while she was gone. I heard her pleading the night before, "Please, don't leave my girls alone, ever. I beg you, Tía Soila!"

She also asked Mamatoya, her mother, to help out whenever possible. They knew that Mamá would never leave her daughters behind unless it was a "life-threatening emergency," like I once heard Tía Soila say. I knew what the words *life*, *threat*, and *emergency* meant, but I had no idea about the whole phrase. Mamá promised Tía Soila that she'd send money home every month as soon as she settled down and found a job.

Later that day, once the family and neighbors heard the news that Mamá had left for the US, about fifteen people, ranging from five-year-olds to eighty-year-olds, gathered at Tía Soila's house demanding more details about Mamá's trip, as if it was any of their business. The whole trip had been a secret. No one knew about it except Tía Soila and Mamatoya.

Sindy didn't even bother to come out of the bedroom to greet everyone when they arrived. She stayed in the dark and Consuelo kept her company. I was on the patio, in the middle of all the conversations. They sat around asking questions and saying things that didn't make sense to me at all. They always quieted down whenever Consuelo showed her face in the corridor. As soon as she would go back inside the room, they continued with the chisme, gossiping about Papá like there was nothing better to talk about.

I listened quietly, pretending I didn't understand. There were some things I did understand, but I continued to play with my sticks and rocks, a naive look on my face. This was the only way I could find out more about the drama between Mamá and Papá.

Sure, I had seen the physical pain they inflicted on each other, but I wanted to understand why. *What happened between them? Between us? Why did we fall apart?*

"Who knows how he's going to react when he hears the news about Victoria," said one. Papá was in the capital, working or getting drunk.

"She had to get away from Raul," said another.

"He was not a good husband," said a random man.

"But Raul loves his daughters!" said a neighbor.

"Last time he drank, he threatened to kill her," said cousin Celia.

Everyone was talking at the same time. I didn't know who was saying what, or why, but all the chisme made me sick. I didn't know what to feel anymore; I didn't feel like crying. I felt a pain in my chest. Like some invisible hands were wringing my insides.

Papá wants to kill Mamá? Is that why Mamá left for El Norte?

I wanted things back to normal. I wanted Mamá there with me.

I didn't want to go to bed without Mamá caressing my face. The day was quickly vanishing. How far away was this infamous Norte everyone was talking about? I couldn't wait to be there with Mamá. She'd promised to come back for the three of us and take us there, to the Promised Land.

Cierta vez caminamos
Junpech xojb'ehik

En lo mas alto del templo de La Danta
Mi gente canta en Poqomchi'

Su flor y canto se origina de las
Montañas más antiguas de Nakbé

Sus proverbios nos alientan
A brotar como

Orquídeas palpitantes;
Luna llena bajo un sexto sol.

Once, we walked
Junpech xojb'ehik

At the peak of La Danta Temple
My people sing in Poqomchi'

Their flower and song come
From the oldest mountains of

Nakbé. Their sacred proverbs
Enlighten us to sprout like

Pulsating orchids—a full moon
Under the sixth sun.

Mayuelas versus Tactic

After Mamá went to El Norte, my sisters and I were left under the care of Tía Soila and Mamatoya. Tía Soila had always lived in Mayuelas, and Mamatoya had begun her new life in Tactic, at the age of twenty-two, without Mamá. Tía Soila and Mamatoya were like the towns Mayuelas and Tactic—night and day. They were two sisters that didn't look anything alike; their actions, thoughts, and desires resembled the moon and the sun.

My mother grew up in Mayuelas. It's always hot and humid there. The summers seem to never end. When it rains, the smell of the wet earth blooms with the humidity. This only attracts more mosquitoes. For the most part, the soil is arid and the dryness becomes even duller, like a ghost left behind by a light rain.

The town of Mayuelas grows old with its people's souls. El río is the only thing that keeps Mayuelas alive. It flows, but it doesn't go anywhere. People are not hungry for education or culture. They barely survive with what they have. Things have not changed much after all these years. Some people have left, and the ones who have stayed behind are still living their lives under the same scorching sun.

Tactic is the complete opposite. It's a small village hidden in the wintry Chama Mountains of Guatemala. It has emerged as a town full of colors, songs, and culture. The fog covers it every morning and evening. The constant rain preserves the evergreen of the mountains and fields, and the rich smell of pine trees fills the air.

Summer feels like it only lasts two weeks in Tactic. The rain mists throughout the day, and at nighttime people fall asleep with the sounds of raindrops exploding on their tin roofs. It is a truly magical place to live. People there speak in beautiful songs, in Poqomchi', the native language of the town's indígenas. They dress in handmade cortes and embroidered huipiles. Their multicolored attire tells our stories—our people's history.

On special occasions, the Moors parade the streets mocking the Spanish conquistadores with their deer dances. This is a special pre-Hispanic dance where men dress up as tigers, lions, monkeys, and deer. They dance on the streets pretending to hunt the deer. The conquistadores' dance represents their victory over the Mayan people and how they converted them to Christianity. But during these dances, the conquistadores are teased and laughed at. They are not taken seriously in Tactic.

In Tactic, even the dead depart content. The street funeral processions are filled with pain, music, incense, and laughter as they make their way to the town's vibrant cemetery. The tombs are painted in different shades of turquoise, lavender, orange, blue, and yellow.

I have always preferred Tactic to Mayuelas, but I prefer Tía Soila to Mamatoya. I lived in both towns the three years Mamá was away in El Norte. We spent a few months in Tactic and a few months in Mayuelas—back and forth. When Mamá's dollars ran out in Tactic, or simply disappeared like magic, we'd take a guagua to Mayuelas, four hours away.

In Mayuelas, Tía Soila never complained about there not being enough money to feed us. She'd always find a way to make the tortillas with salt and limón last longer and taste better. But Mayuelas's heat was intolerable. I embraced the cold weather of Tactic; I even learned to tolerate the coldness of Mamatoya's home. This is where I learned the true meaning of hunger, and not just the literal one.

Mayuelas, on the other hand, will always be Mamá's home. This is where she wants to be buried. Even though I prefer Tía Soila to Mamatoya, I already know that I want to be buried in Tactic.

Nuestro fruto

Ella se encaramó
En las ramas más altas
Del árbol de tamarindo.

Lo hamaqueó con todo
Su ser hasta hacerlo
Llover flores—

Flores tiernas
Que nos dieron
De comer.

Tía Soila

She elevated herself
On the tallest branches
Of the tamarindo tree.

She rocked it with all
Her being until it
Rained flowers—

Tender flowers,
Raining down—
On us.

For Tía Soila

I remember Tía Soila being dark and thin. I can still picture her hiding a pack of cigarettes in one of her hollow apron pockets. Her hair was white. I have this image of her in my head: she's resting on a rock by the river, piles and piles of people's dirty clothes sit in front of her while she calmly combs her long, straight, raven-black hair, parted down the middle. Now it looks like soft snow melting on her shoulders.

When I was little, living in Mayuelas, I remember Tía Soila rocking the tamarindo trees to sell the fruit in the mercado. She was thin, but strong. She never married. At a young age, she birthed two sons by different fathers. She raised both of them by herself. Danilo and Osvaldo live in the US now.

I once heard Mamá say that Tía Soila went through menopause in her early thirties. She has always been alone ever since I can remember, but she has never complained or been afraid. Tía Soila is a vibrant, special being.

She also used to be a sholca; she had lost most of her teeth due to gum disease at the age of twenty-five. The few teeth she had left bothered her to the point where she yanked them out by herself, one by one.

Her toothlessness never stopped her from smiling or talking to anyone who crossed her path. She was a sholca until her late forties when Osvaldo, her eldest son, bought her a set of brand-new teeth. She refused to wear her dentures for the first couple of years, until she finally gave in. Got used to them, I suppose.

I remember how she would struggle chewing meat. She'd take forever to swallow. I remember asking her when I was eight, "Tía Soila, would you like me to chew the food for you so that you can swallow it more easily?"

Everyone at the dinner table almost choked laughing. She laughed uncontrollably, her thin body shaking. Tía Soila was a proud woman, regardless of her missing teeth. She walked on the arid streets of Mayuelas triumphantly, with an erect, thin back and the sweetest smile—the size of a plantain.

She had always been thin like a toothpick, smoked three to five cigarettes a day, drank Gallo beer with her meals, played poker with her male friends, and sold números—the pueblo's weekly lottery.

Even though Tía Soila was illiterate, she was self-sufficient. She sold lottery tickets on the street. She taught herself how to read and write numbers one to one hundred. She memorized these numbers—the way they looked, the way they sounded.

Every Sunday night, she listened to a radio station that announced the winning number for the week. She prayed that no one had bought the winning number, so she could keep all profits. Sometimes she had to borrow money from neighbors and friends to pay the winner when she didn't sell all hundred numbers, or when her sons forgot to send her money from the US.

Before learning how to sign her name with a pen, Tía Soila signed with her left thumb. In time, she learned how to print the five letters of her name: S-O-I-L-A. When I enunciate her name slowly, it sounds like *soy la*—"I am the." Or sometimes if I say it too fast, it sounds like *sola*—"alone."

La Siguanaba

Tía Soila's ranchito was a one-room hut with an adobe wall in the middle. This wall divided the room into two: the bedroom and the kitchen. The kitchen was made of adobe walls and the room of cement blocks. The dining room was outdoors next to the patio and was covered with a tin roof. The floor was made of soil. There was no bathroom, only an outhouse a few yards away, up on a hill, next to the tallest tamarindo tree.

I loved eating the tamarindo's fruit, breaking the crisp auburn shell to get to its soft and stringy sour meat. Tía Soila prepared a sweet drink with the fruit to cool us off on hot summer days. We call it fresco de tamarindo.

I was brave enough to use the outhouse during the day, but never at nighttime. The flying cockroaches hiding on the dark walls around the cement toilet bowl were bigger than my head.

During the day, I forced Tía Soila to go with me and scare them away. At nighttime, I learned to hold it, most of the time. Tía Soila couldn't stand the smell of a bacinilla under the bed. So if I ever had an emergency at night, I was forced to pee on the patio while Tía Soila held the flashlight in her hand to scare the spiders and toads away.

But there were other things in my mind that Tía Soila couldn't scare away. With the light of the moon, Tía Soila stood out in the shadows of the mango and tamarindo trees wearing her long white camisón. I didn't like looking at her because she reminded me of la Siguanaba, with her long hair and white nightgown.

I grew up hearing two versions of la Siguanaba. According to Mamatoya, la Siguanaba was a beautiful woman who wandered the streets in the middle of the night. She lured men with her beauty. But when they approached her, she revealed her skull face and drove them insane. She was a spirit, a madwoman.

Tía Soila told us another version of la Siguanaba. Her version was the one that scared me the most when I was little, especially at two or three in the morning when the patio was pitch-black.

According to Tía Soila, la Siguanaba also appeared to children. She would tell us her scary stories at nighttime, whenever she would hear strange noises coming from the toma, the water canal that surrounds her house. This was her way of keeping us off the streets at night. It also kept Sindy away from the canal, where her admirers would visit her.

"La Siguanaba had children of her own, but she drowned them and abandoned them in the river," Tía Soila would say to us while we lay in bed in the darkness.

Every night I slept in a different bed. Sometimes I slept with Consuelo, other nights with Tía Soila. Sindy slept with Consuelo whenever I slept with Tía Soila, and Consuelo slept with Tía Soila whenever I slept with Sindy. It was like playing musical beds.

"She usually takes the appearance of the child's mother in order to charm them and take them away," she continued.

"What does she want with them, with us?" I wanted to know, holding on to Consuelo's hand. Our hands were clammy, but I wouldn't let go.

"She leaves them stranded in the woods near the river," responded Tía Soila.

I always wondered if la Siguanaba knew that Mamá had

immigrated to the US and if she would ever pretend to be her. How would I tell them apart?

Tía Soila would take only a flashlight with her every time I had to use the bathroom at night. I was too embarrassed to ask her to bring along her machete, the one she used for chopping firewood.

Tía Soila told me that one way to scare la Siguanaba away is to bite the blade of the machete. I don't think I could ever find the courage to bite Tía Soila's dirty machete. I usually go limp when I get scared. I never believed that making the sign of the cross upon la Siguanaba would do the trick to scare her spirit away. That was Mamatoya's way of getting rid of her.

Finally, one night, I couldn't take it anymore and bravely told Tía Soila to either wear another camisón or put her hair up because she reminded me of la Siguanaba. She exploded with laughter as we went back inside the house. Her laughter confused me even more, but she never wore her white camisón again.

En el olvido

Cántaro rojizo de barro vivo,
Llegaste a la vejes quebrantado
De tanto olvido.

En tu cintura
Yacieron flores grabadas
De matices tiernos—

En tu boca abundó:
Agua oscura, agua sagrada, agua
Que todos sorbimos sin piedad.

Forgotten

Red cántaro, of vibrant clay,
You have arrived at an old age,
broken, from so much neglect.

At your waist, etched flowers
Were born of soft shades—
In your mouth, dark water,

Sacred water, flourished;
Water which we all drank
Without empathy.

Mayuelas's Mill

That afternoon, like every afternoon at the mill, we formed a line to recount the latest rumors and scandals of the entire town. Everyone went to the mill with their bowls filled with grains of tender, freshly cooked maíz. At five p.m., this was the place to be.

The mill had the loudest engine in town and the power to grind all the people's cooked corn into fresh masa.

As I waited in line, I would toss a handful of cooked kernels into my mouth like buttery popcorn and watch the live soap opera unfold before my eyes. The stinging cal, the powdered lime, had not fully drained from the grains of the maíz in my bowl. But this was how I enjoyed eating them in order to savor their salt.

The noise from the mill's motor was piercing. It forced us to yell at the top of our lungs—as if people didn't have any other place to get together and relate their sorrows or condemn the latest Fulanita who had given birth to a lovechild.

Every day, some type of drama occurred at the infamous mill. A possessive mother dragged her daughter by the hair for taking more than the allotted time to run an errand. A lesbian, or a marimacha as Tía Soila called them, slyly grazed her unsuspecting love interest's forearm while waiting in line. And poor Doña Dolores, after yet another deportation from El Norte, once again took her place at the end of the line.

"Dolores, you're back!" the mill conductor greeted her.

"Not for long, Ricardo," she replied.

"Make sure to say goodbye the next time you leave us again," he smiled.

At exactly five o'clock, the mill magically converted the maíz into smooth, fresh, freckled dough. Later in the evening, Tía Soila would prepare the tortillas by hand so that my sisters and I could eat them with salt and a little bit of limón.

Eating tortillas with salt and lime was truly a privilege for us when there were no more beans and sour cream. This was the case whenever Mamá's dólares ran out, but Tía Soila never complained or treated us badly. This was the difference between Tía Soila and Mamatoya.

I was almost ten years old and very much aware of my surroundings and the struggles of the people in Mayuelas, but what worried me the most at the mill was the five seconds allotted to us by the operator for us to scrape the trapped dough from the mouth of the grinder.

This monster, the mill, was powered by electricity. It was made of steel and had two mouths. One sat on top of the motor, patiently waiting to be fed grains of corn. The operator's job was to add water to the top mouth so that the sharp plates, or its teeth, would grind the corn and turn it into soft dough. The dough would come out at the bottom of the other mouth, where it would sometimes get trapped.

Scraping the trapped dough from the mouth of the grinder was my worst nightmare.

I was afraid that my fingers would get cut off if I took too long to scrape out the leftover dough. It had happened to too many girls before.

I was afraid that my broken bowl wouldn't be full because of the dough I might leave behind.

I was afraid that the town's people would notice how this

monster, the mill, intimidated me even though I always pretended to be brave.

My legs trembled every time my turn approached.

Full of anxiety, we placed our fingers inside the mouth of the grinder with a pressing need to scrape the dough from the blades of the motor.

Although the concealed dough was often not even ours, we would quickly gather it and force it into our broken bowls.

Dalia, the girl in front of me, thought she was quick and agile in scraping her dough out. But in my eyes, she did not fully utilize the five seconds that the operator allowed.

Better for me, I thought.

The last thing I wanted to do was steal someone else's bloodstained dough. I did not have the heart to combine the dough and pretend that nothing had happened that afternoon just to withstand the force of hunger later that evening.

But, unfortunately, I did not have the option to waste those precious seconds. I had to take advantage of my time and even scavenge what Dalia had left behind. I left a little bit of me behind in the blades of the mill, but no one noticed.

That night, I had to bite my tongue in order to not reveal to those at the dinner table the reason why the tortillas—fresh from the comal—gave off a light, rosy complexion. We ate in silence.

La Familia

Mamá was the oldest of six siblings: four girls and two boys. Anita, Sandra, Carmen, Edwin, Mario, and Marleny. All six of them were her half siblings; they all belonged to Don Lalo, the man who despised Mamá, the man who married Mamatoya when Mamá was only six.

Tía Anita

Anita was the second oldest, but I don't know much about her because she passed away when she was only six years old. She died of typhoid fever and no one in town knew how to help her. Everyone who met her still remembers her green doll eyes. I got to see the transparency of her eyes in a black-and-white photograph Mamatoya kept on her bureau.

Tía Sandra

After Anita passed away, Tía Sandra became the second oldest. She is four years younger than Mamá. I have heard many stories of Tía Sandra, and I believe them all. She laughs at everything even when things are not funny, not even for a six-year-old.

She dropped out of elementary school in the fifth grade. But she enjoys reading the newspaper every day.

Tía Sandra had two kids—a boy and a girl. Mayra and Randolfo were my youngest cousins at that time. Randolfo is one year younger than me, and Mayra is two years younger. They are exactly one year apart; coincidentally they share the same birthday month and date: May 28.

Tía Sandra believed she wasn't meant to be a mother. Thank

goodness she tied her tubes and only had two kids, because Mamatoya ended up raising her children. Both Randolfo and Mayra call her by her first name, Sandra. Mamatoya has been their mamá ever since they can remember.

Tía Sandra was the type of aunt who had mastered the art of annoying us, especially me at the age of seven. She thought I was the cutest thing she had ever seen, with light skin and giant brown freckles spread over my face. Every time my sisters and I would return to Tactic from Mayuelas, she would bury my face in her stomach. That was her way of hugging me. She would grab both my cheeks and kiss each one, saying, "You're back, abispita." Then she would throw her head back laughing nervously, nonstop. I never understood her laughter back then.

Carmen, Tía Negra

Tía Negra is Mamatoya's fourth daughter and her favorite child. She was quiet, reserved, intelligent, cultured, and beautiful. She was the only one of the girls to graduate from high school. She even took some courses at a community college thirty minutes away from town. She was granted a visa at a young age and traveled to the US often.

We all respected her because she spoke differently from everyone else in the house. She had a sophisticated accent, the type of accent that only teachers and the wealthy people in town had. The rest of us had a singsongy accent, according to the neighbors.

La Negra, as we all called her, was the only one from the whole family who landed a job as a bank teller, a well-respected job in Tactic. And because she was the only one in the house who had a full-time job besides Don Lalo, she always bought us little gifts every year for Christmas and at the August fair, where we got on all the kids' rides like the ferris wheel, the merry-go-round, and the bumper cars. She made sure that we all had a good time at the fair even if we only got to get on one ride or play lotería once. La Negra was good at saving money. She hid a giant piggy bank in her closet. No one knew about it except for me because I'd slept in her room and shared her bed.

Every so often when I was left alone in her bedroom, I would sneak into her closet and would turn her piggy bank upside down and shake it. Through the little opening slit, chocas would land on the floor. I would run to the store by myself with the twenty-five cent or ten-cent coins and buy pan dulce, ice cream, or a Coke. My stomach would always hurt after eating or drinking her money. Somehow I managed to never get caught.

Tía Negra was always well liked by the people in town. She was the only one of us who got invited to social events because she knew how to behave. She attended church every week and sang in the choir. She was soft spoken and blushed every time she gave away one of her smiles. As quiet and painfully shy as she seemed to be, she loved to sing like a bird of paradise at parties and at church. She even participated in the town's singing contests every year. I don't think she ever won, but everyone applauded her and adored her for her gentle personality. She was my favorite aunt besides Tía Soila.

Tío Edwin
Tío Edwin was Mamatoya's fifth child and the first boy. He was only one year younger than Tía Negra. They were like

twins, inseparable. They had the same introverted personalities and were the only two out of the seven siblings to graduate high school. Tío Edwin had a good head on his shoulders just like Tía Negra.

But they looked completely different: Tío Edwin was light skinned, had light brown hair with green eyes. Tía Negra had straight jet-black hair, olive skin, and dark brown eyes, the shape of almond seeds. They loved each other deeply.

Tío Edwin wanted to be a lawyer. He was in his last semester at the Universidad de San Carlos de Guatemala when he passed away. He was diagnosed with cysticercoids, a tissue infection caused by eating food or water containing tapeworm eggs. He suffered throughout his college years. He almost went blind. He had several brain surgeries, and his seizures continued until he finally passed away. Tío Edwin had a promising life.

Every year in December, when Mamá was gone, he would take my sisters and me to the forest to choose the Christmas tree. We would choose the tallest and prettiest pine tree. Tío Edwin never said, "It won't fit in the living room." He simply chopped the tree with an ax, and we would help him drag it back home. The whole family would get together to decorate it. The tree shimmered and twinkled with different-colored lights and homemade garlands and ribbons. It looked full of life even though its top was usually bent because the living room ceiling wasn't tall enough. But the pine aroma would inundate the house. We all loved Christmas time.

Tío Mario
Tío Mario was Mamatoya's sixth child. He was the first one

born in a hospital; her previous children had all been born at home with the help of a comadrona, a midwife, as was customary to do in those days.

Mamatoya had complications while giving birth to him and was rushed to the nearest town's hospital. According to Mamatoya, the doctor pulled Tío Mario out of her womb by tugging on his right leg. His leg never recuperated and somehow became longer than his left one. He had a distinct limp that everyone could recognize miles away.

Mamatoya never accepted that one of her son's legs was deformed.

"Mario is not my son," she would say.

She accused the doctors and the nurses of exchanging him for another baby. Yes, Tío Mario still has a hard time accepting himself because Mamatoya always finds a way to tell his story at every family reunion. Tío Mario is only four years older than me. Mamá says that he's definitely family because I act just like him—like a complete clown that doesn't take life seriously.

Tía Marleny

Mamatoya gave birth to Tía Marleny when Mamá was two months pregnant with Consuelo. That means that Mamatoya and Mamá were both pregnant at the same time for two months. Tía Marleny is Mamatoya's youngest child.

Tía Marleny is short and tubby, with green eyes the size of giant, transparent marbles. When she was five years old, she caught a sinus infection that never went away until she became a mother. She always had a hard time breathing through her nose, producing green and yellow mucus nonstop.

Randolfo, Mayra, Sindy, Consuelo, Marleny, Mario, and I

grew up together. We attended the same elementary school. Sometimes we were all placed in the same class and grade level.

We all made fun of each other, but we especially ganged up on Marleny. We called her all sorts of names: mocosa because of the yellowish-green boogers always dripping down her nose; vizca because one of her eyes had a mind of its own, which made her appear cross-eyed; janana because of her nasal, squeaky voice. We were cruel kids.

Marleny hated school. She repeated first and second grade twice. When I began first grade, I was placed in her class with Profesor Freddy. I was seven years old, and she was already ten. We both made it to second grade with Seño Chaty, the infamous teacher who wore a mask of makeup and always scratched her butt cheeks whenever she passed in front of our house. We all mocked and imitated her mannerisms, especially Mario.

I moved on to third grade while Marleny repeated another year in second grade. She dropped out of school when she finally made it to fifth grade.

She of course wasn't the only fifteen-year-old in the history of Eriberto Gomez Barrios Elementary School to drop out of fifth grade because she had to repeat it. School wasn't for everybody. She simply gave up on education and had no choice but to stay home and help Mamatoya sell homemade food from door to door, from business to business.

Mario had already given up on school the year before. They were the youngest siblings, and since they had quit school, Mamatoya forced them to roam the streets of Tactic selling delicious food and appetizers like enchiladas, tostadas de frijoles, and rellenitos. Mamatoya was a great cook. Everyone in town knew it.

Mario would usually make Marleny sell to neighboring stores full of hungry people, while he hid a block away. They were both ashamed to do the job. Edwin on the other hand not only helped Mamatoya with the cooking but also gladly volunteered to sell it on the street. Hundreds of people attended his funeral. He was well liked by the town's people just like Tía Negra.

Tía Marleny also automatically became Mamatoya's caretaker. The youngest daughter who never marries or leaves the house is destined to care for her aging mother. She didn't have a choice, at least according to Mamatoya.

Don Lalo

Don Lalo married Mamatoya when Mamá was six. He never liked Mamá since the very beginning. He didn't like us, either. He was a thin, Indigenous man born in Tactic. His German hazel eyes enticed Mamatoya to leave everything behind, including her daughter, my mamá.

When Mamá was in the US, Don Lalo always complained about the noise level or the mess we created in his house. He hardly ever spoke to us. He worked long hours as a security guard for a large coffee plantation. He was gone for weeks at a time. Whenever we did see him, he was always drunk.

I only witnessed one physical fight between Mamatoya and him. He was drunk that day, and Mamatoya beat him up with a broom and buckets of ice-cold water. He never dared touch her again.

T	where would she be
H	tonight if she wouldn't
E	have taken her on that
P	winding path—
E	tied her tiny hands
R	behind that broken
S	wooden chair—
I	hidden her beneath
S	the bridge to Gualán—
T	shattered her screams
E	into silent rain while
N	eating her soul away?
C	would she be alive today
E	avoiding the smell
O	of evergreen moss
F	found in the riverbed
A	or the familiar
N	(unfamiliar) distorted
I	face of a stranger
G	smiling her way?
H	would she perpetually
T	drink her silence
M	like bitter melted
A	ice and carry on
R	convincing herself that
E	nightmares don't exist?

Little Devil

I was eight years old when I had my First Communion in Tactic. My mom sent me a beautiful white dress from Los Angeles for this special occasion. I looked like a bride, ready to marry the first boy who tickled my stomach with the blink of his eye.

The truth was, I was terrified by the undeniable scent of incense that oozed through the cracked adobe walls of the church. Each wall was filled with effigies resembling people that didn't look anything like us.

The crucified Jesus Christ at this church was light skinned, unlike the black Christ resting in Chi-Ixim's temple, located on a hill twenty minutes from Tactic. All the saints in Tactic's church had European features—tiny noses with thin lips—unlike my sisters and I and most of the Indigenous people in town. Only the Ladinos, who were half Indian and half Spanish or from German descent, were fair complexioned and had hazel or blue eyes. My skin was pale compared to Consuelo and Sindy's, but I still had my Mayan nose, dark almond eyes, and big lips. Consuelo's nose was just like mine, except she had bushy eyebrows. Sindy had dark, curly hair and a dark complexion.

Listening to the dramatic songs and prayers that echoed along with the organ chords shattered my composure. Then I remembered why I had been so excited to do my First Communion: I wanted to taste the famous wafers after mass. I wanted to form a long line in the middle of the pews and pretend to be a virtuous girl. I wanted to be like most people in town: good citizens. I didn't know what I was getting myself into.

A few minutes before the ceremony, Mamatoya reminded me that everyone in Tactic was a devoted Catholic. We had no choice but to do our confirmation. As Mamatoya covered my face with my transparent veil, she asked me, "Are you ready to confess your sins to Padre Alfredo?"

"What sins?" I asked. I felt my face burn with my big fat lie.

"Before you receive Communion you have to confess everything to Padre Alfredo so that he can absolve you from your sins. Then you can enjoy the wafer," she said.

"What's *absolved?*" I asked.

"He forgives all your travesuras," she said, smiling.

I wanted to cry. How could I tell Padre Alfredo my secrets, my sins? I realized that I was never going to taste the famous wafers that melt in your mouth. That's how my older friends described it. I never understood why some people simply sat on the pews instead of forming line to get Communion.

On that day, things began to make sense. They probably had too many painful secrets to confess to Padre Alfredo. I sat quietly on one of the pews to gather my memories, good and bad, behind my veil before proceeding to the confessional booth.

I was four when I committed my first sin.

It was a hot and humid day in Mayuelas. That afternoon, Mamá came back from the market, sweating and in a bad mood. She didn't even bother to say hi to me. She ran to the bathroom to shower with cold water. She locked the door behind her, leaving me outside. I whimpered like a sad puppy. I was used to taking showers with her, but on that particular day, for some reason, she was furious.

I stood outside the door, peeking through the keyhole. As

she undressed, I noticed she covered her private parts with her palms. She knew I was outside. Before getting in the shower, she unlocked the door to let me in. I sat on the floor watching her from behind the shower curtain.

"What are you hiding, Mamá?" I asked.

"Don't ask dumb questions!" she shouted.

I became more curious as she soaped her slender, muscular body. I could see her through a hole in the shower curtain, but she caught me and scolded me again, "Stop staring, abispa. Don't be such a naughty girl!"

I was only four, but I felt like the dirtiest four-year-old in the whole world.

I was four and a half when I committed my second sin.

I fell in love with one of Mamá's older friends. His name was Omar. He would visit us once a week to play poker, smoke cigarettes, and drink with Mamá and her other girlfriends. I became obsessed with Omar. I often dreamed of him, naked, flying like an angel.

Instead of a penis, Omar had a white paloma that fluttered its wings incessantly. My whole family and everyone in town call the male penis a paloma, a dove. I'm not sure why.

In my dream, Omar rose in the air like Jesus, and reaching with both his hands, said, "I love you, Claudita."

The next day, I was so excited about our love that I told the entire family about my dream.

"Omar me ama!" I shouted, jumping up and down. They all laughed in my face.

"Omar is in love with me," I tried to convince them.

Mamá sat me on her lap, hugged me, and said, "Ay

sompopito, Omar is just a family friend and he likes you as such."

I continued to make a fool out of myself. "No!" I said. "Omar is in love with me!"

The phrase *No Mamá, es que Omar me ama!* became famous among family. I never forgot Omar.

I was five when I committed my third sin.

These experiences did not traumatize me. They did quite the opposite. I wanted to know even more about people's bodies and why they covered and hid certain parts from me.

I remembered one time when Papá came home from work complaining about a pain he felt in his paloma, his penis. I was in the kitchen with Mamá trying to flip some tortillas on the comal. My parents spoke in Gerigonza, Pig Latin, so that I wouldn't understand them. Little did they know that I had learned Gerigonza at the age of four, on my own. I knew *pafa-lofo-mafa* meant paloma.

Even though Mamá was under the impression that I didn't understand what they were talking about, she kicked me out of the kitchen. I was forced to go to the patio to play by myself because Consuelo and Sindy were at school. From the patio I saw them go into their bedroom. This just inflamed my curiosity. I wanted to see Papá's white dove—I was obsessed. I wanted to see how Mamá cured his paloma with her magical cream.

I stood outside their bedroom window, plotting away. The bedroom had two windows. There was an old wooden table between the windows, against the wall. I pushed the wooden table underneath one of the windows and climbed on top of it. Then I began jumping up and down trying to reach the window. As I jumped higher, I chanted, "I want to see Papá's paloma, I want to see his white dove!"

What I really wanted to see was if Papa's dove fluttered its wings the way Omar's did in my dreams. I wanted to see the exact moment when Papá released his paloma to be free. At the age of five, I never really understood why boys kept their doves caged in their pants. *No wonder they get sick,* I thought.

But I couldn't see anything. Mamá's curtains were too thick to see into their bedroom. I stopped my chanting and sat on the ground instead. I began to cry realizing how the poor dove was going to suffer in there. I never saw it leave Papá's cage.

I was six when I committed my fourth sin.

All my childhood memories came to me fresh and raw a few minutes before the ceremony. Doing my First Communion began to feel more like a trial: good versus evil. I was afraid to fail the test. Another of my many nicknames was diablita—little devil.

Mamá was a social butterfly when she was younger. I remember the day she visited one of her best friends, Alba, who lived on the other side of town. Alba had a five-year-old daughter who loved to play with me. Her name was Ceci.

Ceci and her mother lived alone in a large house that practically had a forest for a backyard. The house seemed empty and lonely, but was surrounded by tamarindo trees, mango trees, lemon trees, and orange trees. It was enormous.

As soon as we got to Alba's house, Mamá let go of my sweaty hand and instructed Ceci and me to play tag in the backyard.

"Alba and I will watch you from here," Mamá reassured me.

They each sat on a hammock drinking their spiked lemonade.

Before running into Ceci's forest, I overheard Mamá tell Alba, "I have to be careful with my diablita. I don't know where she gets it."

"She inherited it from you, mujer, who else?" responded Alba.

Laughter shook their bodies while they sipped their lemonade. Their voices faded away as Ceci and I got lost in her backyard. We found the perfect spot to play pretend house behind some bushes. It was too hot to play tag like Mamá had told us.

We played for hours. At least that's what it seemed like because I really just wanted to be with Mamá and Alba.

"Why can't they make us a pitcher of sweet lemonade?" I asked Ceci.

She didn't respond, and I quickly got bored. At some point, I don't know how it happened, but I heard Mamá shouting my name, and calling me other names. I was a pícara, a diablita, and a cerotuda—a little turd. I was the worst mischievous six-year-old girl alive, according to her.

Mamá and Alba were far away from us.

Did they see us? I thought. I had only been curious whether Ceci had a panito like mine, or a paloma like Omar in my dreams.

Ceci got scared and nervously pulled her panties up and took off running to hide behind her mother's skirt.

I did the same and I ran behind her, tormented by the nonstop insults Mamá spat at me, one after the other.

"Ichoca jodida, you dirty brat!"

When I finally reached them, Mamá and Alba busted out

laughing. I froze, not knowing what to say or do. I felt lost, like I was walking blindfolded on the surface of the moon.

I was seven when I committed my fifth sin.

Mamá began having serious talks with me when I turned seven.

"No one has the right to touch your panito, do you hear me? If someone ever does, you let me know and I'll take care of it. You understand, sompopito?"

I promised Mamá that I would never let anyone touch my private parts. I guess she was preparing me to take care of myself because that was the same year she was forced to immigrate to the United States, leaving my sisters and me behind.

When my sisters and I moved to Mamatoya's house in 1985, we all shared her home with her children and grandkids. We all grew up together as if we were cousins. We called each other by our first names. We all played together on the street, inside the house, and in el potrero, the forest across from our house. We played everywhere and everything we could imagine: fútbol, hide-and-go-seek, tag, school, with the river's clay, with fire, with water; we flew kites against the wind. I was seven and Mario was eleven years old, almost a teenager.

One day while everyone was at school, I stayed home pretending to be sick because I hadn't finished my homework. I was terrified of Profesor Freddy, my first grade teacher. He would hit students with a ruler for not turning in their homework.

Before Mamá left, no teacher ever laid a hand on my sisters and me. No one dared.

On that day, Mario didn't go to school, either. Mamatoya

and Tía Sandra were running errands in el mercado. I was home alone with him. It was rare to see the house empty. There was always someone there, but that morning, the house was completely still and silent.

Since I wasn't really sick, Mario and I decided to play bicycle tag inside the house. We couldn't play outside because my school was a few yards away, literally across the bridge. I made the game more interesting by having him tag me while riding his bike. It was tough to maneuver the bike even though the house's corridors were long and wide. Eventually, he got tired and told me that he wanted to play something else.

"What do you want to play?" I asked.

"Let's pretend to be novios," he said. Boyfriend and girlfriend.

I didn't think anything was wrong with his game until he wanted us to kiss on the lips. When he moved his face toward mine, I turned and kissed him on the cheek and ran to my room to hide. He didn't come after me.

At least I didn't let him touch my panito, I thought to myself.

We never spoke about it, like it never happened. At the age of seven, I had a boyfriend who happened to be my tío.

I was almost eight years old when I committed my sixth sin.

It had been almost a year since Mamá had left for El Norte. When we were in Mayuelas, I was free to roam like an abispa searching for the sweetest nectars in the tallest tamarindo and mango trees. I had complete freedom to spread my pollen on the dusty roads that led to the river; at the grassless school yard; at the mercado sipping on a twenty-five-cent banana milkshake; on the street playing electrizado, tag; at Tala's molino, grinding the maíz for the tortillas; at the toma, wading in its muddy waters to cool off; at my second cousins' who lived next door. These were all the places I could visit on my own when I was seven and a half.

There was only one place I wasn't allowed to visit or play in: the small hut between Tía Soila's house and her brother Tío David's house. Mamá forbade me to enter the hut, but she was no longer there to scold me if I disobeyed. When my great grandmother died, Tío David and Tía Soila inherited most of the land. They divided the land in half and built their homes next to each other. The hut was exactly in the middle between both houses. Mamatoya had married young and moved away to Tactic long ago.

The abandoned hut was in the middle of the patio surrounded by mango, grapefruit, jocote, lemon, nances, granadilla, and tamarindo trees. It had been there since I was born, but I never dared to enter it because it was dark and isolated. People said that someone had died inside once. The only ones allowed in were Tío David's children. He had five: two older daughters, Celia and Mery, who were about Sindy's age; Carlos and Jorge, who were four and five years older than I; and Lesvia, the youngest, who was only three years old. She was known as "the accident."

While Mamá was gone, Sindy, Consuelo, and I began to spend more time with our second cousins in Mayuelas. We played at their house, and they often bathed with us in the river. Celia was eight years older than me. She had already celebrated her quinceañera. She gave me extra attention for being the youngest; she was kind.

One day, when we were coming back from the river, our

clothes drenched, Celia asked if I wanted to change in the little hut. I didn't want to go back home, even though it was practically next door. I wanted to spend more time with her. Celia was daring; she wasn't afraid of anything. And I was also curious to go into the hut. I wanted to see what it looked and smelled like. I never dared to go in there alone, but with Celia, I felt bold and special.

Sindy and Consuelo headed back to Tía Soila's house to change; they were soaked and didn't care to see the inside of the hut. I stayed behind with Celia. The hut was dark and thick with dust. It didn't have electricity. Celia opened one of the back windows to let in some light. My eyes adapted quickly and I was able to see my surroundings. I remember everything being blurry like a discarded, unfocused photograph.

"Here," she said and handed me a clean shirt and some cut-off shorts that were long enough to cover my knees. I took off my wet clothes and changed in front of her. I gave her my back. She also undressed but didn't turn around. I couldn't help but notice her breasts; they were big. They looked like two tennis balls stuck on a fence. She was a beautiful girl and she knew it. She smiled at me and didn't bother to cover herself like Mamá had done when I was four. I noticed her long, dark hair framing her tiny waist. Her body was slender and muscular just like Mamá's. I blushed and looked away when she looked me in the eye. As soon as she was dressed, we went back outside, where my sisters and cousins were waiting for us. We were ready to play another round of electrizado. But as hard as I tried, I couldn't erase Celia's breasts from my mind. I felt dirty.

The next day, Celia invited me back to the hut. I didn't have to say anything. I understood the look she had in her eyes.

After sitting around for a couple of hours, chatting and doing practically nothing, everyone went their own way. Celia purposely stayed behind to talk to me. As soon as everyone was gone, we went into the muggy, dusty hut.

We didn't talk much. We simply sat in the dark. The heat and the quietness of the hut made Celia take off her shirt and her bra. I stood there like a statue with my big eyes fully dilated; I wanted to let as much light in. We were in the hut for only a few minutes, but it felt like months. I began shaking. Without saying a word, I took off running to Tía Soila's house; I felt dirty and scared again.

But I went back the next day. I couldn't understand why I wanted more. Celia had inexplicably turned into a drug. We had a routine and this routine lasted a week. We had our own language to communicate: our eyes. All of us kids played together outdoors, but as soon as everyone parted ways, Celia and I stayed behind to enter the hut. I never took off my clothes for her.

On the seventh and last day, she took off all her clothes and asked me to lie next to her on this tiny, dusty bed. I didn't know what to say or do. I simply shook nervously. The hut was quiet and still. All the dust had settled. I did as I was told. I was fully dressed.

We lay next to each other on the corner of the tiny bed. Within a few minutes of silence, she grabbed my hand and put it on her bare breast. The hut got even quieter. Slowly, small particles of dust began floating in the air and the walls began to creak.

"Don't worry," she whispered, "the hut is settling."

I closed my eyes. In the darkness, behind the redness of my

eyelids, I sensed a long prickly hair on her breast; I had the urge to pluck it, but I froze. I couldn't stop trembling.

We were face to face when I felt her left hand slide inside my pants. I quietly went insane with pleasure. I felt dirty and guilty simultaneously. I closed my eyes again and Mamá's words came to me in a flash: "No one has the right to touch your panito. If someone ever does, you let me know and I'll take care of it."

I couldn't believe I had broken my promise to Mamá. I quickly got up, shook the dust off my clothes, and ran outside to find the rest of the clan. I felt my cheeks burning, but no one noticed. That was the very last time I entered the hut. I never told anyone, especially Mamá because I knew what she was capable of doing. Sometimes I would bump into Eufemia in the village and notice the scars Mamá had left on her face.

As the days passed, Celia tried to invite me to the hut with her quiet eyes. I never went back, and we never spoke about it. It was true what Mamá had said about me: I was a dirty little girl, a diablita with two horns sticking out of my head and a tail between my legs. But the real diablita was Celia. She was older than me. Good thing Mayuelas's heat became unbearable and my sisters and I moved back to Tactic. It was then that Mamatoya enrolled us in catechism classes. A few months later I was doing my confirmation.

There I was, sitting on the pews, waiting for my turn to visit the confession booth for the first time. Padre Alfredo was young and very good looking. He always had a long line of young women wanting to confess their sins to him; I didn't want to confess mine.

I wasn't sure which sins I was going to fess up to. The girl in front of me stepped out of the confessional booth. She seemed relieved. She walked over to me and knelt on the pew. She began to recite Our Fathers and an Ave Maria—a Hail Mary.

I stood up and slowly walked to the booth. Padre Alfredo was inside the tiny box, sitting behind a rectangular, small window. I couldn't see his face through the window screen. I immediately crossed myself as I knelt before him. I stood there for a few seconds trembling until Padre Alfredo finally asked in a soothing voice, "Do you have any sins to confess, hija?"

During First Communion classes, one of the nuns had trained us to say, "Forgive me, Father, for I have sinned," or "I accuse myself of the following sins." Both statements didn't make sense to me at the time. Confessing my sins was not part of my plan. So I told him half the truth. "Padre Alfredo, please forgive me because I'm a sinner." These words came out of me vibrating fast from my chest. I wasn't sure where to start. I didn't want Padre Alfredo to know my wicked ways. So I lied.

From behind the confession booth's little window I heard him ask again, "What are your sins, hija?"

"I lie all the time. I have a dirty mouth." And before he could interrupt me, I continued, "I have also seen and touched things that I'm not supposed to."

I could tell Padre Alfredo was tired. Twenty-five children were celebrating First Communion that day. He had already absolved twenty-four sinners before me. I was the last one, and he was tired and bored, openly yawning. He didn't bother to ask me what kind of things I had touched or seen. He simply said, "I absolve you of your sins in the name of the Father and of the Son and of the Holy Spirit. Recite three Hail Marys."

I did as I was told. I recited the three Hail Marys. Soon

after, Padre Alfredo stepped out of the confession booth and invited all of us to line up to take the Communion wafer. I immediately got up and joined the line. I was one of the first ones.

When Padre Alfredo put the wafer in my mouth, I promised myself to do three things: to never allow anyone else to touch my panito, to never look at a naked body again, and . . . the wafer melted in my mouth before I could think of a third promise.

Tactic's River

Every Tuesday at three p.m., I had my routine. Well, better yet, my godmother's maid was the one who had the routine. I would just observe her as she walked down the hill in front of Mamatoya's house. Like a roly-poly, all curled up from my corner, I could see her through the veranda's railing. From the darkness, I patiently waited until she crossed to the other side of the river and until she came back to the top of the hill. She never caught me spying on her.

It was well known that my godmother was a wealthy woman in Tactic. She had two sons and one daughter, who she spoiled by buying her everything she wanted. Every Tuesday, their maid passed in front of Mamatoya's house to the other side of the river with two to three bags of trash. Mamatoya had already forbidden me from going to the garbage dump, where the maid threw away all those little treasures I so desperately wanted.

But every week, I found a way to escape Mamatoya's scornful stare. I was an agile and precocious eight-year-old. I would climb the wall of the dump like a professional rock climber, even though the cement wall was twice my height. Every time I jumped the wall I would land on the spongy, moldy surface of the trash dump. And somehow, I always felt an undeniable guilt. But at the age of eight and a half, that's where I wanted to be, immersing myself in that penetrating smell.

Carefully, I would squat in the waste so that no one could see me; it would be embarrassing to Mamatoya if anyone saw me. It was a fact that Mamá was away and that we were poor, but Mamatoya reminded us that we should always have dignity, and we should always be clean even though we were poor and needy.

At the dump, I found little treasures that others discarded. And the most valuable keepsakes I found were always the ones my godmother's sixteen-year-old daughter threw away. Every week there was something different: a bottle of scarlet-red nail polish, a gold-orange lipstick, a broken eyeliner, or a hair clip. I risked a good scolding or an ear pulling for those treasures.

The aroma from the dump was sharp and pungent. We came to know the smell very well since we were next-door neighbors. That aroma impregnated my nose and hair, my skin. I swam through the waves of garbage finding toys to entertain myself.

When the majority of the townspeople had voted to build the dump next to the river, Mamatoya and our neighbors protested to the local authorities, but it was all in vain. The dump was still built right next door to us. Other people who lived miles away argued that it needed to be built for the benefit of the river. I liked having the dump close to my house, two houses away to be exact. The garbage dump kept me away from the river.

The river was the only thing that entertained me before the dump was built. I would make paper boats and let them float, sink, or disappear in the river. I gathered fresh clay from the river's walls and created my own toys out of clay. I even fished in that river, but Mamatoya would never let us keep or cook the fish. I did everything in the river except swim in it. My friends didn't swim in it either because the water was fresh from the mountains—it was freezing. The river was also known as río negro.

Every time our ball went into the river, all of us kids gathered to figure out a way to rescue it. I never went in to retrieve a ball. It wasn't the cold water that prevented me from entering the river, but the vivid image of Mamatoya throwing trash into it in the middle of the night, saying, nearly toothless, "Why do they want to save this river if it has always been and will always be filled with shit—shit that the fish eat, and shit that others consume after gutting them."

I've never been able to forget that image. And her resentful words still resonate in my mind. That was exactly what prevented me from entering the river. Unfortunately, her words never stopped me from secretly visiting the garbage dump—I have the same rebellious blood that runs through her.

Speaking of Robbery

That morning I knew I was going to have to work twice as hard to earn my lunch money at school. There were only forty-five minutes left until recess. Mamatoya couldn't afford to give us money, not even five lens, a nickel, for an ice cream. I'd always felt hungry ever since Mamá left for El Norte. When Mamá was home, we were treated with respect. No teacher ever dared to yell at us or hit us at school. Kids came to our house to play. But things changed when she left.

By second grade, I was already famous for the little jobs I did in order to buy snacks during recess or lunch. I was sometimes paid as much as one choca, twenty-five cents. In order to do these jobs, I would finish my classwork before everyone else. I copied chalkboards full of notes.

Two of my classmates, Laura and Luisa, were lazy and spoiled. They never finished their work on time. They knew they could get away with anything, not just because their parents were teachers at school, but also because they could always rely on their Sunday allowance to pay for my labor. Of course, they preferred the latter to feel important and powerful.

But I was like a fox; I had my wits and never allowed anyone to take advantage of me. I wrote contracts out for each one of them. My penmanship was impeccable, and I jotted down what felt like a thousand words per minute.

"I have an idea," I said to them.

"What is it?" asked Luisa.

"I'll copy your notes from the board before the recess bell rings," I said.

"How much do you want?" asked Laura.

"Two chocas from each of you," I said.

"Only fifty cents?" Luisa laughed.

"Yes, unless you want to pay me more!" I said sarcastically.

"No, it's fine," said Laura.

"And you promise that you'll finish before the bell rings?" asked Luisa.

"Yes, you have my word. You'll get to go out to recess," I reassured them.

In those times, a choca was a fortune for a nine-year-old girl whose mom's monthly US check was never enough to feed fifteen other mouths in the house. But for my wealthier classmates, a choca was joke. Their parents would give them five quetzales of allowance per week. They were spoiled millionaires, but I couldn't complain because by the time recess arrived I had already earned one quetzal, and it would last me a whole week. I would run out to play at recess, triumphantly, with four chocas in hand and blisters on my fingers.

Some lucky days, I would even get invited to one of their houses to play. Luisa took pity on me and invited me over after school. I was dying to see her new toys from the US. She had a house full of them. Every summer she went on vacation to New York with her family and brought back boxes full of toys—you'd think she'd bought the whole store.

Her house was a child's paradise. I had never seen anything like it. She had a dark blue mini-sofa where I fit perfectly; I was practically skin and bones. She sat on the edge of it, half of her butt in the air. Luisa loved showing off her toys and each of their functions to me. I was fascinated.

"What's this?" I asked, picking up a plastic rectangular box.

"Put it down! It's an Easy-Bake Oven. Papi bought it for me on his last trip to Los Angeles."

"Aw, Los Angeles," I repeated, not because I was impressed, but because that was where Mamá had been living for almost a year and a half. I missed Mamá.

I wanted to play at Luisa's house every day and bake cakes in her mini-oven. Luisa was an only child and her parents treated her like a princess. She had terrible mood swings, but I always knew how to get on her good side. I simply agreed with whatever she said, and she shared everything with me. I always followed Mamá's advice to the tee: you have to know how to lead a mare to water.

Luisa was also known to be greedy, and she always had candies hoarded everywhere. She was in a good mood that day because she shared some exotic candies with me.

"Want to try some sweet-and-sour candy?" she asked.

I nodded. She placed the powdered candy in my mouth. I was too intrigued to ask her what flavor it was. I wanted to take advantage of her charity before she changed her mind.

My stomach had never experienced these candies. They were clearly not from Guatemala. The small packages with sweet powder came in every flavor and color imaginable. Luisa had them all and in abundance. Those candies were like a drug to me. I got addicted, and a little no longer satisfied me.

I don't know what came over me, but as soon as Luisa let her guard down, I hid a candy in my jeans' pocket. We spent hours playing with her toys while I was suffering from withdrawal. I couldn't take it any longer and with a desperate tone told her, "It's getting late. I have to go home."

She rolled her eyes and said, "Not yet. Just wait!"

I didn't want to get on her bad side, and I knew that if I didn't obey her she would never invite me back to her house.

We left all the toys to one side and started to play the choo-choo train game.

"You're the pilot," she said. "Here, blow this whistle."

I did as she said. She wanted me to be the pilot—I was her pilot. She wanted me to blow the plastic green whistle—I blew the whistle.

I got anxious and soon enough began to sweat. With an improvised tune, I pretended to be the locomotive.

"I'll be the caboose," she said as she grabbed onto my waist.

We chugged along for a few minutes around her room. I was too busy with the whistle in my mouth that I didn't notice when Luisa slipped her hand in my back pocket. When I finally did feel it, I simply closed my eyes. Her deafening cry penetrated her bedroom's thick walls.

"My candy—you filthy thief!" she yelled. Everything felt like it happened in slow motion. I was left with no other option but to flee. I ran all the way home, crying. My tears were hot and thick with shame. I had never been in the habit of stealing, and much less getting caught!

At Nightfall

I scrub my body to the bone.

—Anna Swir

Every night, she quietly   undresses
           in the darkness of her bedroom. She
places her tired flowered dress in the family's
armoire, built with one-hundred percent   uncured

wood. As she hangs it up,   she contemplates:
every wrinkle,   every tear   it gains each year.
In her hands, it becomes   thin   like paper,
silky and soft   from so much wear.

The following day,   she selects a different layer;

she selects another   dress.
(the freshest   one,   the lightest   one)
The one   that will help her survive
the battles of this dream—

                this life.

Mamá Returns

After three years of going back and forth from Mayuelas to Tactic and from Tactic to Mayuelas, Mamá came back to her homeland. She came back for us, just like she had promised.

Tía Soila always said, "Your mother has a backbone like no other woman."

Mamá had returned for her three daughters, her greatest treasures in life. I was already ten, skinny as an earthworm. My hair, light brown, was cut short above my ears—it made my freckles stand out like tiny brown fleas scattered on my Mayan nose. I was as pale as a grieving ghost.

Consuelo had already turned twelve. She was fair skinned, not too dark, not too pale. Her long, dark brown, shaggy bangs covered her bushy Frida eyebrows.

Sindy was eighteen. She was already a señorita, flaunting her jet-black, curly hair; her large curls gracefully accentuated her dark complexion.

Mamá looked different to me, shorter and thinner. She smelled different, too. A scent I did not recognize—a flowery perfume from Avon, perhaps. Her lavender smell had vanished. She wore shiny, three-inch heels with skinny jeans. Her hair was still short, dark brown. She didn't wear much makeup, but her lips were plump and red like always. She barely smiled. She looked almost the same, except prettier and somewhat happier.

When I read Mamá's letter stating that she was coming back to Guatemala, I imagined the day of her return to be the happiest day of my life. I pictured her waiting for me in the middle of Tía Soila's corridor holding two suitcases. As soon as she saw me getting home from school, she would drop her bags on the floor, run up to me, hug me, and carry me like an infant bundled in her arms. It didn't happen in that sequence.

For one, I saw Mamá at the airport and wanted to jump on top of her and kiss her face and smell her hair. I had missed her so much, but I had nothing to say. No sound came out of my mouth. I was surprised at my shyness toward her. I had developed a joker's personality to cope with her absence.

Sindy and Consuelo were laughing and crying, thrilled to see her again. Mamá didn't cry. I stood still, trying to hide my face in my neck. Since I didn't find the courage to approach her, she walked up to me and hugged me tight. She buried my face in her soft yet firm belly and said, "There you are, my sompopito!"

She didn't mention anything about how big I had grown in the past years. How my face was looking more like a teenager's. She didn't notice how my freckles were slowly fading from my face. "Let's get out of here," she said, grabbing her luggage. Mamá disliked being in airports and the capital. It made her nervous and anxious. She wanted to go back to the heat of Mayuelas. During our four-hour commute, Sindy and Consuelo kept asking Mamá questions about Los Angeles and Amado. I usually got carsick so I sat quietly in the back admiring Mamá's beauty. She sounded different, more sophisticated. As soon as we arrived in Mayuelas, all I wanted to do was hold her in my arms, never letting go.

But Mamá didn't allow me to climb her body like a mango tree like I used to when I was little. Mamá didn't allow me to kiss or suck her cheeks like a tamarindo pit. She kept her distance, not just from me, but from everyone else, too. Mayuelas was always hot, but on that day, it felt like a cold winter afternoon. And I felt like a mango forcefully detached from its tree. Not ready, not ripe.

I got nervous realizing I couldn't climb her like a tree or eat her kisses like a fruit. Confused, I ran to the outhouse holding my stomach. I hid in there for twenty minutes, holding my nose. Everyone else continued to gather around Mamá like she was a famous rock star. In the outhouse, I couldn't cry, I couldn't laugh, or scream. I sat on the toilet for a few minutes, pooping, thinking, wondering who she had become. I wondered how much I had changed in her eyes. How many times did she die in the fall and resuscitate in the spring? Three times. Three years to be exact.

Then it finally hit me—Mamá was back. I wanted to tell her how much I had missed her and loved her and needed her. I pulled up my underwear without thinking or wiping my behind and carelessly ran outside and rushed at her.

I jumped on her and wrapped my legs around her waist. We almost fell. I cried, she cried, we all cried, again. She held me tight for a few seconds, but suddenly I felt her body go limp.

As she let me go, she scolded me, "Go wash your hands, you smell like shit!"

Everyone's cries turned into laughter. I ran to the washbasin crying, laughing, realizing Mamá was really finally back.

PART II

OUR JOURNEY TO EL NORTE

Tejiendo la niebla

Descalzo uno emigra
a tierras extrañas

hay quienes no olvidan;

hay quienes se ensartan
su patria en el alma.

—La tierra no tiene fronteras
murmuran los pies reventados

las huellas que implantan
trasmiten nostalgia;

hay tierras calientes
que a veces se enfrían;

hay campos dorados
que tejen la niebla;

hay volcanes que arrojan
sus piedras de pomo;

y uno aquí, escupiendo
cenizas en la lejanía.

—La tierra no tiene fronteras
suspira la arboleda.

El árbol exiliado no logra evitar
que su fruto florezca.

Es el viento que arrastra a
la almendra y la hace que
engendre en tierras ajenas.

Knitting the Fog

Barefoot, one immigrates
to foreign lands—

There are those who
do not forget;

Those who interweave their
motherland into their soul.

The soil knows no border,
murmur their splintered feet.

Their footprints, deep-rooted,
radiate with nostalgia.

There are warm soils that
at times become frozen;

Golden fields that
blur with fog;

There are volcanoes that
expel rocks of pumice.

And I'm over here, spitting
ash from afar.

The soil knows no border,
moans the green forest.

The exiled tree cannot prevent
its seed from flourishing.

It is the wind who drags
it to foreign lands where
it inevitably propagates.

Northbound Again

The day Mamá decided to bring my sisters and me illegally to the US, Tía Soila told us with a stern voice, "Your mother raised herself on the streets. The streets made her tough. She is who she is because she's had a rough life. Be good to her."

Those were her last words as we boarded the guagua that would take us to the capital, Guatemala City. I was ten, Consuelo was twelve, and Sindy was eighteen. Mamá had always been strict with all three of us. I knew she loved us, but she hardly showed her affection to us or to anybody else. Her silent love had always been enough for me, especially at nighttime when she caressed my hair until I fell asleep.

"Life made you hard, Victoria," Tía Soila said to Mamá through the bus window.

Mamá simply nodded her head. We each felt a knot of pain stuck in our throats. We swallowed it in silence and cried all the way to la capital.

Mamá chose a chilly morning to begin a new chapter in our lives. For the second time, she boarded the same bus that had taken her away from us three years earlier. But this time, she was not alone; she had us, her three mujercitas.

After a year of residing in the US, Mamá had fallen in love with a man named Amado. She married Amado, whose name literally translates into beloved. Amado helped my mother settle down in the US. He helped her financially and emotionally. It was thanks to him that Mamá found the financial support to return to Guatemala for us.

Amado was twenty-five years old, and Mamá was thirty-three. Amado had no children of his own, and Mamá already had the three of us. My sisters and I were eager to meet him. Everyone said grand things about the famous Amado.

In her monthly letters, Mamá would describe Amado as a kind angel sent to her from heaven. He was gentle and hardworking; he had no addictions and loved Mamá unconditionally. They are still married to this day.

Mamá couldn't bear him any children because she'd tied her tubes after giving birth to me. This never bothered him. According to Mamá, Amado was eager to meet us and treat us like his new daughters.

I couldn't wait to meet Amado. I had seen pictures of him. He was short and thin. I could tell he really cared for Mamá because in the photos she sent us, he was always holding her gently by the waist.

The funny thing is, Amado also happens to be from our town, Mayuelas, but Mamá and Amado never crossed paths there. They met for the first time in Los Angeles. The night before our trip, I kept hearing his name everywhere.

"Oh Amado, he's such an angel!"

"Victoria is such a lucky woman to have found a man like him."

"He's going to be a great father to the girls."

I couldn't believe I was going to meet my stepdad in a few days. I was excited and a bit jealous. For some odd reason, I couldn't picture Mamá with another man. I'd spent the last three years without a father figure. Tía Soila and Mamatoya had raised us in a matriarchal environment.

I hadn't seen Papá since the day Mamá left for the US. He never bothered to check up on us or visit. He'd also immigrated to the US, chasing after her. He didn't find her right away. And when he did, Mamá was already married to Amado. And now, I was going to meet this amazing Amado that everyone seemed to love and know so much about, except me.

The night before we left, Mamá had made special pockets in her underwear's cotton panel. She folded large bills of quetzales and tucked them neatly inside of them. As I watched her, I fretted she would have an accident and get the money wet.

"Just in case we get robbed," she said nonchalantly.

That morning on the bus, as I said goodbye to my relatives, I cried like I had never cried before. I cried because I was leaving my family. I cried because I was leaving the country of my birth. I cried because I did not know if we would ever come back. I cried because I didn't know if we would reach our destination.

Only the company of Mamá and my sisters gave me the strength for the long journey ahead. For the third and last time that morning, we said goodbye to Tía Soila, Mamatoya, and the rest of the family through the guagua's dirty, broken windows. We simply waved our hands and cried quietly inside the bus.

Meeting the Coyote

We undertook a journey that took twenty-one days. I had no idea that the first bus we took was headed to Guatemala City, la capital. I was naive to think that the bus would take us straight to the US where Amado would be waiting for us in our new home. Nobody took the time to sit me down and explain the rules or what the plan was.

We spent four hours on that bus, standing in the aisle, crying the whole way. When we finally arrived, I was disappointed to find that we hadn't even left the country. Those hours had felt like an eternity in my ten-year-old head.

As soon as we got off the bus, Mamá said, "We need to find the coyote."

"What do we need a coyote for?" I asked, confused.

Mamá ignored me and continued to hold my hand while she searched for the "coyote."

Why do we need a coyote? I kept asking myself.

"Aren't coyotes dangerous?" I asked again.

"Claudita, please stop asking questions," said Consuelo. "Mamá is nervous right now. Don't get under her skin. I'll explain later when we have time to rest." She whispered in my ear so that Mamá wouldn't get edgy.

"That's him," Mamá assured us.

"Who?" I asked again. I covered my mouth right away recalling what Consuelo had said.

"How do you know that's the coyote, Mamá?" Sindy asked.

"Over the phone, he mentioned that he would be wearing a white cowboy hat. Wait here," Mamá instructed us.

She walked up to the man wearing the white hat. She

wanted to confirm that he was really the one she'd made the deal with.

In those few minutes that Mamá was gone, Consuelo told me that a coyote was a human trafficker.

"The coyote will smuggle us across the US border from México," she said.

"Smuggle?" I asked, unsure of what it meant.

"To move us illegally into the United States," said Sindy.

"Illegally?" I tried to make a joke, but the girls ignored me.

Mamá motioned us to come to her to meet the coyote. The coyote was not at all what I had imagined. He was a tall, thin man who wore tight blue jeans, cowboy boots, and his white hat. He introduced himself as Javi.

Javi seemed eager to shake Sindy's hand, but Mamá didn't give him the opportunity to even look at her. I could sense that Mamá disliked him. I didn't trust him, either. I don't know what was it about him that rubbed me the wrong way. It could have been his tight blue jeans or perhaps his leather cowboy boots that made him appear taller than he really was. Javi felt our mistrust for him, so he cautiously guided us to the park where a larger group of people from all over Central America were gathered. We all had the same intention to cross illegally to the other side, El Norte.

The group was composed of older men and women, young girls, and children. The young girls would get nervous around Javi. Javi flirted back with them. He would wink at them while delivering his instructions. The way he winked at Sindy bothered me. Mamá didn't take it lightly, either. From the get go, she put her foot down and made it clear that he should stay away from Sindy.

"Don't you dare wink at my daughter again, you understand?" Mamá scolded him in front of everyone.

He nodded and put his head down, letting the shame sink
in.

Tapachula

Javi's instructions were clear and simple:

Pretend you don't know each other.

Keep some distance from the coyote and from each other.

Don't talk to strangers or stray off the road.

Everywhere you go, pretend that you're on vacation.

We did exactly as we were told. Before dispersing into small groups, another coyote approached Mamá. This coyote was the opposite of Javi. He was older and had a thick mustache. He was short and chubby. He introduced himself as Marco. He wasn't interested in checking out Sindy or Mamá. He had a serious face, and I felt safe around him.

"Why can't he be our coyote?"

"Shhh!" Sindy hissed, reminding me to keep my mouth shut.

Marco gave Mamá some documents. She put them in her purse right away. All these things were happening right in front of me, and I felt lost. Confused.

"What did the coyote give you, Mamá?"

"¡Nada, don't worry about it!"

Then Javi came over to our group pretending to be a tour guide and said, "Please follow me. I'll be your guide for this trip."

We each carried a light backpack with only the most essential clothing items. I always kept my thick sweater tied around my waist. Mamá carried a large purse under her arm and a small amount of cash handy. The rest of the money was hidden in her underwear. As we began walking I felt scared, but Mamá held my hand tight. Consuelo and Sindy walked behind us. We kept our distance from the rest of the group. We stuck together like a pack of wolves.

That same day in la capital, we boarded another guagua that took us toward Tapachula, Chiapas—México. We were fortunate to sit together. Mamá made sure of it. She pleaded with a couple to trade seats so that both Consuelo and Sindy were behind us.

Marco didn't board the bus with us. Javi sat in the front talking to a young woman from El Salvador. She was beautiful and wouldn't stop laughing at his jokes. I couldn't hear anything he was saying, but his facial expressions were animated and comical.

A few minutes later, I began to feel sick from watching the trees pass by my window at seventy miles per hour. I fell asleep on Mamá's lap. Three hours later, we arrived at Tapachula.

Tapachula felt immediately like home, as though we had never stepped foot into another country. As we walked through the central park, I looked at the shoe shiners, who were just patojitos, small children, who had grown strong perhaps too quickly. We were the same age, but I knew we were different. At home, I would go to school and play marbles, freeze tag, or fútbol with my friends. I didn't have to shine anyone else's shoes.

The streets were filled with hawkers. The singsong shouting routines of the street vendors rang in my ears as they tried to convince each passerby that they were selling the most innovative goods from another world. They were selling anything from sunglasses and purses to food. The food smelled good. I was always hungry.

The streets were also filled with music and laughter. I could hear marimba jingling in the distance; I was delighted by my surroundings and foolishly pointed to Javi, who was discreetly guiding us from a distance.

"Look Mamá, there goes the coyote!"

Mamá had no choice but to squeeze my hand, hard enough to silence me the rest of the way.

We were a small group of ten people: the four of us, the pretty Salvadoran girl with her mom and little brother, an older couple, and a single man. I wondered who or what this man had left behind. Was he traveling alone like Mamá had done three years earlier? If he'd left his children behind, I hoped he would go back for them just like Mamá was now doing for us.

Javi was in charge of our group. The first thing he did was to take all of us to a flophouse in the outskirts of Tapachula. I had never stayed in a flophouse before. We hardly traveled as a family. We only went back and forth from Mayuelas to Tactic and once in a while to la capital, where we usually stayed with Papá's family.

Our first night in Tapachula had no moon; it was cold. Our flophouse room was just like the rooms in Mamatoya's house, except Mamatoya's rooms were spotless. This room had four dirty purple walls, two windows, two twin-size beds, and a metal door. I slept with Mamá, and Consuelo slept with Sindy. One of the windows didn't have glass, just some iron bars that apparently didn't convince Mamá. She kept her eyes open all night. The next morning, my sisters and I woke up with swollen bites, bites from mosquitoes that had easily come through the barred windows. Mamá had dark circles under her eyes.

Getting to Know Javi

The next day, early in the morning, our group gathered in front of the flophouse. Javi brought everyone scrambled eggs and tortillas. He called them burritos. I immediately pictured eating a donkey wrapped in a tortilla. While we devoured our burritos, Javi gave the adults instructions on what to do next. I stayed behind with the girls, trying to eat their leftovers.

"He's kind of cute, isn't he?" said Sindy.

"Not really." Consuelo giggled.

"Who?" I asked.

Both ignored me, making it seem as if I was too young to understand their girly conversation about boys.

Then Mamá came up to us and said, "We're going—get your stuff."

"Where are we going now?" I wanted to know.

Again, they ignored me. Javi was walking behind us and overheard.

"We're going back to the bus station where we plan to board another bus that will take us to Oaxaca," he said, winking at me this time.

Mamá didn't notice. I looked back and smiled at him. Mamá noticed that and squeezed my hand. I was beginning to like Javi. He wasn't such a bad guy after all.

When we got on the bus, there were no more seats available. Javi stood up and offered his seat to Mamá.

"Sindy, sit here and let Claudia sit on your lap," said Mamá.

Sindy's face turned all sorts of colors. It went from pink to red to purple. No matter what color her face turned, she did not look in Javi's direction—at least not in front of Mamá.

Sindy took a seat and I sat on her lap. Mamá stood in the aisle, holding Consuelo's hand, keeping Javi away from Sindy and me.

Sindy hugged me and buried her face in the back of my neck. I could sense her giggling and feeling important. Sindy had a crush on Javi. She didn't mind that my hair was sticky and smelly; I hadn't showered in two days.

"I love you, abispita," she whispered through my short, tangled hair. I'd never felt so special.

When a few people got off the bus, Mamá and Consuelo found a seat in the back. A few minutes later, the lady sitting next to us across the aisle got off. Javi didn't waste any time. He immediately snatched her seat. He didn't care that the pretty Salvadoran girl was still standing in the back of the bus aisle, holding on to the luggage rails.

I was starting to feel sleepy, but I didn't want to miss this for anything in the world. Sindy's hands got clammy and began to tremble. She could sense Mamá glaring at them. But there was nothing Mamá could do from back there.

Javi was desperate to talk to Sindy, but Sindy wouldn't look at him. I kept smiling and winking at him, playfully. He smiled back at me and said, "Why do Guatemalans laugh three times when they hear a joke?"

"I don't know," I said, shrugging my shoulders. Sindy kept quietly looking out the window. She pretended to be distracted by the sky and its clouds.

Javi continued with his joke, "Once when it's told, once when it's explained to them, and once when they understand it."

I pretended to understand the joke and laughed a hearty

laugh, holding my stomach. Sindy couldn't help but laugh, too. Javi and I kept laughing throughout the trip. My laughter was so loud that it traveled to the back of the bus. A few seconds later, Mamá touched Sindy's shoulder and said, "Go sit in the back with Consuelo."

Sindy got up and Mamá took her place. I sat on Mamá's lap and soon fell asleep. Javi had no choice but to keep his jokes to himself.

A few hours later, Javi instructed us to get off the bus. The group gathered in front of a street taco stand. I was hungry again. Mamá bought us each two chicken tacos. Then she warned us not to talk at all. "Mexican people recognize our Guatemalan accent. It's better not to speak, even among ourselves," she reminded us.

What accent? We all speak Spanish, I thought. But I didn't say it out loud. I didn't want Mamá to pinch my hand for the gazillionth time. I ate my tacos in silence.

The Art of Peeing

We traveled from city to city riding on buses. Most of the time I slept to avoid getting carsick. The night caught up to us riding on the third bus. The road was dark. I couldn't see any stars in the sky. We rode on that bus for six consecutive hours. Three hours into the bus ride, I began squirming around. I had to pee badly. I almost cried keeping it to myself, until I finally mustered some courage to tell Mamá. She laughed and handed me a plastic bag.

"How am I supposed to pee in a bag?" I complained.

"Easy. Pull down your underwear, bend down, and open the bag with both of your hands. The bus isn't going to stop for you to go out and pee!"

I was relieved that the inside of the bus was pitch-black, but once in a while, the bus driver would turn the lights on to check up on the people sitting or lying down in the aisle. I was petrified thinking that he might turn the light on right in the middle of my bathroom scene. I didn't want Javi to see me under such humiliating circumstances.

Thankfully the bus driver kept the inside of the bus nice and dark for me. I followed Mamá's instructions perfectly.

"Here you go," I said, handing her the bag after I was done. Mamá tied a knot and set it on the floor next to me. The bag resembled a water pillow filled with orange Tang.

I fell asleep again on Mamá's lap. When I woke up, the bag was gone. I noticed that the floor was moist. Suddenly, a sharp odor of cooked corn infiltrated my nose. I could recognize that smell miles away. I hoped the people sitting on the floor didn't get wet with my bish.

Sindy's Choice

The next morning, we arrived in Oaxaca. It was raining. The streets were empty. We stayed four nights in different flophouses. These flophouses resembled jails with barred windows, no curtains, and sometimes no glass. I knew well what a jail looked like after that night with Mamá. Most of the rooms had the mattresses on the floor. They were dirty, empty rooms filled with fleas and other pests.

During the day, we weren't allowed to leave our rooms unless we had to go to the next flophouse. Javi would bring us food, usually chicken tacos, tortas, or sandwiches. At nighttime, Mamá would take out a few quetzales from her underwear and exchange them for pesos the next day.

The coyotes, Javi and Marco, had planned the course of the trip carefully. Any time we weren't traveling or moving from flophouse to flophouse, we waited as all the groups who were coming from other regions of México gathered. Our group kept getting larger as we got closer to our destination.

One day, when we were all together, I counted up to thirty-five people. But the numbers changed every day, sometimes more and sometime less. People would come and go. I'm not sure what happened to everyone I crossed paths with on our journey. I often wondered whether they arrived safely to the other side or changed their minds and went back to their countries.

Meanwhile, during the day, Consuelo and I entertained ourselves by playing hand games, singing, or reading magazines or newspapers left behind by the last guests of the flophouses. Consuelo would read us the newspaper. In one of the sections, she read about the Guelaguetza Festival that was held in July—it was already August. The last two Mondays of July were special days, known as the fiesta de lunes del cerro.

"Too bad I missed the dancers with their colorful trajes," I said. I pretended I was a tourist on vacation, visiting exotic places and meeting new people, just like Javi had said to do.

Sindy slept a lot, still sad and angry for leaving Guatemala behind. Mamá had practically forced her to come with us. I remember the night we were packing, getting ready for our trip, how Sindy had begged Mamá to let her stay.

"I don't want to immigrate to the US, Mamá," she cried.

"How can you expect me to leave you here? It broke my heart to leave you behind three years ago. I can't do that again. My heart won't take it," Mamá cried back.

"But what am I going to do there? I'm already eighteen. All my friends live here! My life is here. I don't want to go, please don't make me!"

Tía Soila, Mamatoya, Tía Negra, and Consuelo were listening from the patio, crying. I was hiding behind the bedroom door listening.

"I want to stay here with Tía Negra," said Sindy. "Please Mamá, I beg you."

Then Tía Negra rushed into the room and said, "Leave Sindy here with me, Victoria. I will look after her. She's like a sister to me."

"Get the fuck out of here, Negra. I'm not leaving my daughter behind again. Not even over my dead body!"

"Victoria, please, leave her here. Sindy's depression could get worse in the US," said Tía Negra.

"So you're the one who's been putting shit in her head.

She's coming with me whether she likes it or not—whether *you* like it or not!" screamed Mamá.

Tía Negra was nonconfrontational. She walked out of the room, tears streaming. Mamá didn't give Sindy the choice to stay, even though she was already eighteen and considered to be an adult.

Throughout the trip, Sindy always suffered from massive headaches. Consuelo and I rubbed her head, trying to soothe and comfort her. I couldn't picture myself living in a new country without Sindy. It would have felt like my hand was missing a finger. I somewhat understood Mamá, but nobody understood Sindy, except for Tía Negra.

"Ouch!" she cried when one of my fingers would get stuck in her curls.

"Sorry, Sindy," I said, kissing her forehead.

Sindy was like a delicate pink camellia longing for her motherland.

"Let's play the missing game," I said to both of them, inventing a new game.

"What's that?" asked Consuelo.

"I'll start. I miss the river," I said.

"I miss Tactic's meadow," said Consuelo.

Sindy was silent.

"I miss the mango and tamarindo trees," I said.

"I miss the pine trees and the Moros," said Consuelo.

"I miss the marimba music," I said.

"I miss Mamatoya's food," said Consuelo.

"I miss Tía Soila's laughter," I said.

Then suddenly, Sindy joined in. "I miss my life in Guatemala!" That concluded the missing game.

In Conversation with a Poem Called: Detachment

A blue-velvety shelter is what I seek before I transform
into something else. Who knows if I will return as an over-

romanticized poem, or simply indifferent like the silence
of the moon. What's left in me, what lingers, no longer

resembles me. As a child, I passively sank too many times
in the river. I wish to go back to my vacant home in

Guatemala to smell the scent of wet, jagged grass; to visit
El Llano where I'd let myself go from the tallest hill, rolling

down, until I'd reach the mouth of Río Chixoy. It was there
where I was confronted with the reflection of a fragmented

face; where I briefly found the scattered pieces of our childhood in the middle of war. Pieces of me, pieces of Consuelo,

pieces of Sindy floating by, not ready to sink. Dear Mother:
I learned to bury your quiet distance underneath a manic smile.

Dearest Consuelo: I meant to be just like you. Maybe then
Mamá would have glanced at me with her honey-colored eyes.

Dearest Sindy: I finally understood why you purposefully
drowned in your inconsolable gaze. Your disappointment

for life—unbearable. Forgive me for not having the courage to understand your pain. I admire you for not wanting to bathe

in my river. Instead, you chose to eat adobe stones from the walls of Tía Soila's home. Today, I'm going back home.

Matamoros and the Moors

Six days later, we were walking the streets of Matamoros, Tamaulipas. It took us almost two and a half days to travel from Oaxaca to Matamoros. We transferred three times to other guaguas, one of which had mechanical problems, and delayed us by a few hours. The waiting was atrocious. Mamá pulled us away from the gathered passengers and away from the road. The cars would pass by at what seemed like a hundred miles an hour.

I spent the whole time in Matamoros in a state of fear because I always remembered los moros, the Moors, from Tactic, when they would take to the streets mocking the Spanish conquistadores, dressing as Spaniards and animals like deer, monkeys, and bulls. These dances were entertaining, but because *matar* means "to kill," at age ten I imagined that the Moors in Matamoros were being killed.

We stayed in several motels in Matamoros. In one motel, all the rooms were overflowing with people. Some sat on the sills of glassless windows, some on the iron rails, others on the sidewalks, while some remained standing, blocking the doorways. These people weren't part of our group, but they were also trying to cross over to the other side.

Mamá became even more serious than she already had been. It was her way of protecting us. One glare was enough to scare away any man who approached us. Nobody dared to mess with Mamá; she had a ferocious warrior gaze. We successfully passed all the overflowing rooms until Javi led us to a tiny room with two other families. Thirteen of us, mostly women and children, shared the place for one night. Javi made sure that there were no men in this room. Even though there were no men present, Mamá didn't allow me to talk to anyone, let alone interact with the other children.

"Do not leave my side."

"Stay with your sisters!"

"You're not here to make friends," she said.

I didn't leave her side just as she'd told me. I didn't make any new friends at that motel or throughout the trip. Mamá didn't trust anyone. She never did and never will.

Once again, Consuelo and I tried to entertain ourselves by playing silly games. Sindy was never in the mood to join in. After playing the copy game, where we mimicked each other's movements, Consuelo came up with the looking-forward game.

"Is it like my missing game?" I asked.

"Yes. I'll start," she said. "I look forward to eating hamburgers in the US."

"I look forward to learning English," I said.

"I look forward to meeting Amado," Consuelo said.

"I look forward to our new house," I said.

"I look forward to going back home," Sindy said coldly.

This is how the looking-forward game ended, and we fell asleep soon after.

The next day, Javi picked up all three families in a van. He took us to another house about two hours away from the motel.

It was our last night in Matamoros, and we stayed in an enormous house with several rooms. Each room was inhabited by at least ten people, two or three unknown families. There were no beds. Each family received an inflatable mattress. The four of us found a way to accommodate each other. Consuelo and I were squeezed in between Sindy and Mamá. We couldn't turn or find room to shake out a numb leg. However we fell asleep in the evening was how we awoke at dawn.

"It's better this way," Mamá said. "We don't want to leave any space for a malicious hand."

Mamá didn't sleep; she kept watch over us. In the morning, she was grumpy and the bags under her eyes were even darker.

The River Never Happened to Me (i)

I used to walk half a mile from Tía Soila's house to the river; I bathed in it pretending to know how to swim.

I was

eight, breathing, eating the constant heat of Mayuelas. The river was my biggest alibi; its muddy path was crowded with

pumice

rocks, verdant ceiba trees, and buried mango seeds. I came across floating mango pits—cracked opened—their

flesh

consumed to the bone. No one noticed their nakedness floating by or sinking to the bottom of the river; I bathed

in the

river hoping to rescue those seeds from drowning alone. On my way back home, I'd jump from rock to rock, trickling

river

and mango seeds everywhere. By the time I'd reach Tía Soila's house, I was dry, as if the river never happened to me.

The River Never Happened to Us (ii)

We walked more than a thousand miles to get to the other side of
the Río Bravo, guided by the coyote's howl. We didn't bathe in the river.

Instead, we floated like thin paper boats, tanned by the sun.
I don't remember caressing the surface of any pumice rock.

I stuck my fingers between cottonwood crevices, their
trunks rooted on opposite sides of the river. We were bound

to eat desert wind; I was ten. When we reached the other
side, we hid behind bushes; quietly, we sank slowly in the mud.

When the coyotes signaled, we walked, no, we ran and our knees
shed broken pieces of mud. No one drowned in the river; no one had to be

resuscitated from the mud. Yet we continued to trickle
shards of mud, as if the river had never happened to us.

My Side—Your Side

Sixteen days into our journey we finally met the moist lips of the Río Bravo, as it's called in México, or Río Grande, as it's called by those who reside on the other side. It was one of the most terrifying days of my life.

I imagined the river to be just like the one where I bathed every day in Mayuelas: filled with rocks and shade from the mango trees, the water clear and sweet. But when we arrived at the riverbank, I was confronted with a wide river, dense with the color of mud, its currents livid. Even the birds flying above the river didn't dare make contact with it, no matter how hungry or thirsty they seemed to be.

"It looks like Mayuelas's river after it's rained for a whole week," Consuelo pointed out.

"What if the boat sinks?" asked Sindy. "I don't know how to swim."

"I'll rescue you, Sindy," I said, trying to be brave and hopeful.

Marco, the other coyote, was also there with another group of people. Javi made it clear to stay away from open areas. He spoke to us hiding behind some dry bushes. It was hot.

"La migra has their eyes peeled for immigrants trying to cross the river," he said.

We hid behind the bushes, listening closely to Javi's explicit instructions on how to cross the river in the aluminum boats that awaited us.

"Step in the boat carefully.

"Once you sit down, don't move or else the boat will sway and sink.

"Leave space for me in the middle of the boat; I will guide it across the river.

"Parents, sit your small children on your lap.

"We have no life preservers, so be safe. We don't want to leave anyone behind."

After giving us his orders, Javi left the group for a few minutes to talk to Marco and the men who owned the boats. We continued to hide in silence. Consuelo held my hand and Sindy's. Mamá was quiet. She looked like she was meditating. Getting ready. Or perhaps she was remembering how she had crossed the same river twice.

Ten was the maximum capacity of each boat—I counted the seats—but Javi and Marco somehow planned to squeeze in twenty of us, like sardines. The boat was dented on all sides. Water was seeping through little holes that were covered with plastic bags.

Finally, Javi gave the order to board the boats. After a few people had boarded ours, Consuelo stepped in and held on to Sindy's hand. I followed after Sindy holding Mamá's hand. They sat first, placing their small bags under their feet. They rested their hands in between their legs. Mamá sat down next to Consuelo and placed her bag under her seat. Consuelo was sandwiched in between Mamá and Sindy. I think she felt safe, or at least she pretended to be. The boat was so full; it seemed to sink if someone sighed. We were like statues, jammed up against each other. I sat on Mamá's lap, without breathing, without looking back.

Javi, being tall and thin, stood in the middle of the boat. He began to pull the boat across the river, tugging on a rope that was tied to trees, rooted to both sides of the river. It looked like a tightrope, but instead of balancing and walking on it, Javi was underneath, holding tightly to it, and pulling it, dragging the boat across. The trees had deep scars on their trunks.

The other side of the river seemed so far away. Its trees looked stronger and healthier, revealing all shades of green. The landscape looked clean, full of promise. I wondered if the water tasted or felt different on the other side. I swore to never forget the sweetness of the water in my motherland.

The river churned angrily around us with its threatening currents. I closed my eyes, knowing that any sudden movement could rob us of our lives. Those twenty-some minutes of crossing, huddled on the boat, seemed to last an eternity— I feared we would never get to the other side. Mamá's hand was clammy, but she held me tight. Sometimes her strength gave me hope. Sometimes it filled me with despair.

There I was, crossing the river, leaving things and people behind—my home, my family, my country. Mamá was taking us to a new, unknown place, somewhere where I didn't know what to expect. Would I forget how to be myself, how to dance or sing the way I did in Tactic or Mayuelas? I was afraid to forget. I was afraid to change. Sindy had already lost hope since the beginning of the trip. I didn't want to feel like her.

Finally when we settled on dry earth, I asked in hope, "Are we in Los Angeles, Mamá?"

"No, we still have a long way to go," she said.

Frontera de mi lado

Caminábamos
con pies derretidos

platicábamos a
p a u s a s

con bocas
pegajosas

selladas
de la sed.

Nuestras miradas
quemadas,

a s u s t a d a s
de ver tanto fantasma/

en lo oscuro
del camino/

en el polvo
de la nada/

hasta
tropezarnos

con los húmedos
labios del río

Río Bravo
de mi lado.

Río Grande
de tu lado.

Ninguno quiso
beber de ese

serpentino
pasaje.

Nuestra piel
tostada

nos abrigó
y flotamos

como
lanchitas

salpicadas
de

agua dulce/
agua salada.

Llegamos
al otro lado:

Tu lado.
Mi lado.

Border on My Side

We walked
with melted feet

chatting in
s l o w   m o t i o n,

our viscid
mouths

sealed
with thirst.

Our
burnt gazes

a f r a i d
to see the ghosts/

in the darkness
of the path/

in the emptiness
of dust/

until we
stumbled upon

the moist
lips of the river:

Río Bravo
on my side

Río Grande
on your side.

No one
drank from

the muted
river;

our bronzed flesh
kept us warm

as we floated
in the water

resembling
small boats

splattered
with

fresh water/
salted water

we disembarked
on the other side—

Your side.
My side.

Are We There Yet?

After the boat ride, we walked for several hours through plowed land. It looked like a desert, but it wasn't. In the distance, there were vegetated fields that glowed with both pale and flamboyant greens. Then, I don't know how it happened, but suddenly, the arid, dusty path came to an end and I felt my legs go weak. They became heavy. My legs were sinking in a thick mud that went up to my shins, but I continued. There was no time to complain or I'd be left behind.

Muddy, all twenty of us reached a wide road where we were instructed to wait for a truck to pick us up. Again, we hid behind some bushes, quietly, attentive, ready to run just in case.

While waiting, I rested and contemplated the beautiful landscape and the aroma that emanated from the moist soil. Gradually, the mud dried, and I shed my old skin like a snake. *A new land, a new life*, I secretly thought.

Half an hour later, a van came by and Javi instructed us to board it. The van transported us to a hotel in Brownsville, Texas. Once again, we were squeezed into the van, leaving us with no room to breathe; everyone recycled each other's warm and thick exhales. The windows were tinted or covered with black paper. I couldn't see anything on the road. No one said a word.

When we arrived to the hotel in Brownsville, Javi gave us our own room. The room was different from the flophouses we had seen in México. The hotel had two big beds with a desk and a lamp. I ran to the desk and opened the top drawer. There, I found a Bible. I took it out to feel its weight. I put it back right away before Mamá yelled at me for touching things that didn't belong to me. The Bible was written in English, and I couldn't read one word in it. I only knew how to count up to five in English.

I was delighted to see that our room had its own bathroom and that we didn't have to share it with anyone else.

"Consuelo!" I yelled. "Come check out the bathroom."

"What is that?" she asked.

"It's a bathtub," said Sindy.

Mamá was busy talking to Javi and Marco in the hallway. The bathroom looked sparkly clean in my eyes. I had never seen a bathtub in my life. At Tía Soila's house, I showered out-doors in the cement washbasin. Mamatoya's house was a little different. Her small bathroom had a large plastic bucket where we poured boiling water and cold water to shower. I didn't need a bucket of lukewarm water for this bathtub; the knobs were magical.

The first thing I did was undress while Sindy and Consuelo lay on the bed playing with the TV remote. I played with the shower knobs for a while until warm water started to run. While I waited for the tub to fill up, I slid from one end to the other like the ten-year-old child that I was. The water tasted like glory. I felt like I was a dolphin at a waterpark, but the spell was broken when Mamá caught me in full slide.

"How could you slide your bare bottom on this dirty tub? You didn't even give me chance to disinfect it!" she yelled.

I stayed quiet. Naked. Those things didn't matter to me at that age, but Mamá wouldn't allow anything to get by her.

We spent nearly a week at the Brownsville hotel. Javi vis-ited us frequently to explain to Mamá the process of forging documents, which we needed to board the plane that would fly us to Los Angeles.

During that week, Sindy didn't do much. She slept and slept. Consuelo and I played indoor games. We pretended to speak English, mixing Spanish words with Poqomchi' words. I felt happy in this strange, clean place. I couldn't wait to see what our new home looked liked. Consuelo didn't show much emotion; she's always been grounded. I could tell Mamá was already used to this lifestyle, but Sindy continued to spiral in her own head. She gave Mamá the silent treatment for forcing her to leave Guatemala behind.

A Flying Bus

Five days later, we were on a plane headed to Los Angeles. We said our goodbyes to Javi, who had been funny and kind. He kept us safe throughout the trip. Mamá finally allowed him to shake Sindy's hand. Sindy smiled a weak smile. It didn't matter where she was at, or who she was greeting or saying goodbye to. She made it seem like her life had just ended. Guatemala was too far for her to return, almost 2,500 miles away.

The plane looked like a flying bus from the inside, full of people speaking in different languages. It seemed like a monstrous beast that took my breath away for a few seconds during takeoff. I giggled nervously, but quietly. I became paranoid. I felt like everyone was watching us. I knew we had entered the country illegally. I knew that Mamá had forged some documents to board the plane. I knew we looked different because of the way we were dressed, the way we spoke, and even the way we smelled.

I was not used to the friendliness and courtesy of the flight attendants. During the trip, I'd learned how to distrust, how to stay quiet, how to not question anything. Mamá had pinched my hand whenever I inquired about any detail of the trip.

On the plane, I refused to talk. I was afraid that I might say something stupid and people would find out that we had come to the US illegally. I didn't want to be sent back after all the hardship we had endured. Mamá would never forgive me. She had sacrificed so much for us. I'm sure Sindy was praying every day for something to go wrong so that she could return to Guatemala, but Consuelo and I looked forward to starting a new chapter in our lives.

Within twenty minutes of takeoff, one of the flight attendants came around to offer the passengers drinks and snacks.

"Would you like something to drink?" she asked me in English. She looked like a doll, with her uniform and pretty face plastered with makeup.

I hadn't understood a word she said, but I knew what she was offering me. I became mute and looked at Mamá for her approval. I couldn't even nod.

"Water," said Mamá.

Mamá handed me a glass of water and a package of salted peanuts. I couldn't even open them. Mamá did everything for me. I was in awe realizing that a flying bus was up in the air and a stewardess was offering me drinks and snacks. *What kind of a world is this?* I wondered. I didn't even know that "water" meant *agua* in English. Mamá surprised me with her English skills that day.

When the plane landed in Los Angeles, another coyote was waiting for us at the airport. This coyote was short and brown skinned, older looking. He approached us and knew Mamá's name. He introduced himself as Benito. Benito had a good sense of humor, too, just like Javi. He was very talkative. He made me smile, but Mamá didn't approve of that either. He walked us to the airport parking lot where he had parked his car. He placed our bags in the back of his red truck. I sat in the front next to Mamá. Consuelo and Sindy sat in the back.

"How did you like the plane?" he asked me, trying to make small talk.

Mamá squeezed my hand, and I knew better than to respond. I simply smiled. Mamá was not a fan of her daughters talking to unknown older men. Benito got the hint and simply drove us straight to an apartment in downtown Los Angeles, playing his loud salsa music.

On the road, I couldn't believe how enormous Los Angeles was. Skyscrapers and cars everywhere, unfamiliar smells, people dressed funky—just like Guatemala's capital. I didn't see Indigenous people wearing colorful cortes or huipiles. Some people were dressed well with a suit and tie, while others wore shorts and sandals. The road was immaculate, clean, and smooth. I didn't see one pothole. Everything seemed to be even and flat. The car felt like it was gliding in midair.

Benito dropped us off in front of a graffiti-vandalized apartment.

As we stepped out of the car, Mamá immediately grabbed my hand, as if sensing my desire to run through the streets, free, like an animal without reins. With a serious gaze, she handed Benito an envelope with the last payment for the trip. He counted the money and quickly took off in his red truck. He vanished in the distance.

"We have finally reached our destination," said Mamá, smiling a victorious smile, just like her name, Victoria.

I was too excited to feel or say anything. In one breath I took it all in: the sounds, the traffic, the road, the lights, the smell of smog, the buildings, the sky, the sun.

"Is this the famous North that everyone longs for?" Sindy asked bitterly.

No one responded. We hugged and trembled together as we cried. We walked together into the apartment complex. I had never seen so many apartments next to each other.

"Is this our new home?" I asked.

"No, this is Amado's best friend's house. We're just meeting him here," responded Mamá.

We stopped in front of a brown, beat-up door. As Mamá knocked, she asked, smiling, "Are you ready to meet him?"

PART III

THE PROMISED LAND

Amado De Jesus Montejo

When Amado opened the door, I was the first person he saw. He knelt down and said in the most sincere tone, "I'm going to be your new dad." His smile was contagious.

I ran into his arms and knew Mamá approved because she didn't pinch my hand or pull my hair for hugging a stranger. Amado was no stranger. I knew deep down that he would take good care of us just like he had done with Mamá over the past three years.

He then proceeded to hug Sindy and Consuelo. He hugged Mamá last. I could sense their deep love.

The Luggage

Every day after recess, I had a routine where I would hide under my desk while Mr. Caprallis, my fourth grade teacher, would work with a small group of students, the rest of the class working independently at our desks. César, my classmate, would sometimes join me underneath my desk only to mock me or say yet another cruel joke about how my new humongous backpack looked like a traveling suitcase on wheels.

"Claudia, hurry up! Your plane is leaving! Look, it left you; it's gone," he'd say. His laughter would burn all over my body.

It had only been a month since we migrated from Guatemala. Mamá enrolled my sister Consuelo and me at Park Avenue Elementary School, three blocks away from our home. Sindy was eighteen, too old to enroll in high school. Mamá signed her up for night school, where she was supposed to learn English.

I was terrified to attend a school where everyone spoke English. My sisters and I were completely culture shocked. Slowly we were getting used to the Mexican culture in our community.

At school everyone treated us differently. The kids never failed to remind us that we were the newcomers who couldn't speak one word in English. And according to them, our Spanish was horrendous.

"Your Spanish is weird!" they'd say.

Nobody wanted to sit next to us during nutrition, when we ate breakfast or lunch. Consuelo had different recess and lunch times because she was a sixth grader. I only got to see her before or after school. I usually sat alone, noticing how everyone spoke and dressed. I kept to myself to stay out of trouble.

I convinced myself that in order to fit in we needed to have the latest style of backpacks. I persuaded Mamá to get us the kind that everyone at school had. These were cute little backpacks that had rollers and a retractable handle. Mamá thought it was a great idea. But instead of purchasing an actual school backpack, she bought us luggage. Mamá's intention was to kill two birds with one stone.

"These are perfect," she said. "You can use them as school backpacks, and when we travel, they can be used as luggage."

The next day at school, everyone stared and pointed fingers at us. We looked more like flight attendants than elementary school girls. The other students couldn't control their laughter. Consuelo and I pretended to be proud of our new backpacks, but deep inside we were dying of embarrassment; our faces flushed red.

"Where are you traveling to this time? Are you going back to Guatemala or Guatepeor?" They laughed. Guatepeor—the worst of Guatemala.

Consuelo and I said nothing in return and walked quietly to our classrooms. We didn't have the language to defend ourselves, and we didn't have the guts to tell Mamá to buy us another backpack.

Little by little we began to adapt to the different subcultures that emerged from the small city of Cudahy. We couldn't complain; we were the minority in a neighborhood where everyone spoke broken English and Mexican Spanish. According to them, we spoke a different Spanish with an accent that distinguished and separated us from them.

Assimilating wasn't hard. I started to erase the Guatemalan *vos* in my conversations. My voice learned the street slang of my classmates. My tongue learned to imitate a forced sing-song that focused on and stressed certain syllables. I became an expert in neutralizing my Central American accent to avoid being mocked by my neighbors and classmates.

But one night during dinner, I accidently said *orale* to Consuelo, which means "okay" in Mexican Spanish. Mamá opened her eyes wide, slapped me in front of everyone, and with a broken voice scolded me: "Don't you ever speak like that in my presence. You are from Guatemala—not from México."

I sat there silently. Burning tears rolled down my cheeks. I didn't know what to think of myself anymore.

The next day, César's jokes about my backpack continued. "Claudia, hurry up! Your plane left you. It's gone." He'd laugh.

Eventually, I learned to neutralize all my accents. I made sure I didn't sound Mexican or Guatemalan. I didn't want to be from here nor there.

K-I-S-S-I-N-G

"Accents are beautiful," said Ms. Maldonado to all of us. We were sitting around her kidney-shaped table reading words she'd handwritten with a purple marker on index cards.

There were four of us: Consuelo and I, and two other siblings, Maria and Yvette. My sister and Yvette were sixth graders and Maria and I were fourth graders. The four of us were the new kids from Guatemala and Nicaragua; everyone knew this at Park Avenue Elementary School. The teachers, the office ladies, and the students knew us well. We stood out like sunflowers on a canvas of red poppy fields.

Ms. Maldonado was my sister's sixth grade teacher. She stayed after school to help us learn English three days a week: Mondays, Wednesdays, and Thursdays. She was from Puerto Rico, and I loved how she rolled her *r*'s in English and Spanish.

That particular Wednesday, I wasn't in the mood to participate in our usual warm-up routine, which consisted of reading words out loud from Ms. Maldonado's vocabulary word box. One of us would flash the vocabulary cards and the rest of us would read them.

"Claudia, why aren't you reading the words? Do you need help?" Ms. Maldonado asked.

"No, I just don't like the way I speak," I said. I looked at the clock hoping it was already 3:30 p.m. It was only 2:30.

"What do you mean? You don't like your voice or the way you enunciate the words when you speak?"

"I don't know how to speak *good*," I said, my vision becoming blurry. "César said that I speak funny! That I don't know how to speak English or Spanish the right way. That I suck at both."

"It's our Central American accent," Maria corrected me.

"What accent, I don't have an accent! I don't even say *vos* to him when I speak to him in Spanish. I only say *vos* instead of *you* to family members."

"Be patient, Claudia. We don't sound like them because we're still learning English," said Yvette.

Ms. Maldonado observed how the four of us discussed why we sounded so different from everyone else in school. It didn't matter if we spoke in Spanish or in English; we sounded different whether we liked it or not.

After a few minutes, Ms. Maldonado said, "Listen to me, ñoñas. Don't tell me you haven't noticed my Boricuan accent? I'm going to have this accent until the day I die. This is me— don't you like me for who I am?" I never forgot her raspy voice and Puerto Rican lyrical tone.

We laughed for a few minutes until I finally asked, "What does *ñoñas* mean? I hope it's not like ñoño from El Chavo del Ocho."

We laughed even more. We had all grown up watching this Mexican comedy sitcom that had reached all of Latin America in the seventies and eighties. Noño was a chubby child character played by an adult in El Chavo del Ocho. We were having so much fun discussing El Chavo del Ocho that we didn't even notice that it was 3:30 p.m. Time to go home.

The next day was like any other school day except for one silly event that happened during recess. All my friends were acting weird. They made a circle around me and danced and sang the K-I-S-S-I-N-G song.

Claudia and Johnny
sitting in a tree:
K-I-S-S-I-N-G.
First comes love,
then comes marriage,
then comes baby
in a baby carriage!

I was clueless. I had never heard this song in my life. Back in
Guatemala, I was used to chanting songs to games such as "El
Toro Toronjil," "El Matateroterola," or "Campanita de Oro." I
didn't understand what this K-I-S-S-I-N-G song was all about.

My classmates laughed and continued to dance around me
until Marisa got inside the circle with me and said, "Johnny
likes you and wants to go around with you."

"Go around where?" I asked more confused than ever.

"Johnny wants to be your boyfriend," she explained in
Spanish.

I broke one of the circle chains and escaped to the bathroom, blushing. It felt like someone had opened a door directly
to the sun and a solar flare had burned my flesh to the bone. I
ran to the girls' bathroom to look at myself in the mirror, to
make sure my face wasn't bleeding. It felt so hot. I splashed my
face with water to cool off as the bell rang. I smoothed my hair
before heading back to class.

Johnny was the cutest boy in my class, and he sat across from
me. Marisa sat in the same group of tables with us, but next
to him. César sat next to me. I automatically became mute to
avoid César mocking my accent. I didn't want Johnny to hear
any funny words coming out of my mouth. Johnny was the

only kid in the class who couldn't speak Spanish. He looked like all of us and his last name was Aguayo, but he couldn't speak a word of Spanish. Everyone was okay with that, and no one made fun of him when he tried to speak to me in Spanish. He sounded cute, but I never laughed because deep inside I loved the way he sounded. He had a gringo accent, and I was okay with it just like everyone else.

During class, Johnny kept smiling at me, trying to make eye contact. I purposely avoided his brown eyes. César was having a bad day. I stayed quiet. Marisa kept writing notes to me in Spanish. She would pass them to César and César would give them to me, bitterly.

"Johnny wants to meet you after school," said the note.

I responded with a simple *NO* in capital letters and gave the note back to César. César crumpled the note and passed it to Marisa. When the bell rang to go home, I ran to Ms. Maldonado's class to meet my sister. I hoped that Johnny wouldn't follow me there. He didn't.

The next day, Marisa made sure Johnny and I became boyfriend and girlfriend. Since we couldn't communicate in English or Spanish, we never sat together during nutrition or lunch, never walked together or held hands, never allowed our lips to make the shape of a kiss.

One thing we enjoyed doing together during recess was playing kickball. Johnny and I were always on opposite teams and usually chosen to be team captains because we were the best athletes in our class.

When we played sports, I didn't have to torture myself speaking and hiding my accent. My agility and speed did all the talking for me. Everyone respected me on the playground, but in the classroom, it was another story. I was a silent tomboy.

Our relationship only lasted two weeks. Johnny moved away to another city, to another school. I was relieved to see him go. We had a farewell party for him in our classroom. Since I didn't even bother to talk to him during the party, he offered one last gesture of puppy love that has stayed with me until this day.

He came to my house after school. My family and I lived in some blue apartments on Clara Street, a few blocks away from Park Avenue Elementary School. Johnny was best friends with Waldino, my neighbor, who was also a fourth grader at Park Ave. Johnny went to Waldino's house hoping to see me one last time. He made Waldino knock on my door and ask for me. Mamá didn't think much of it because Waldino and I played together in front of the apartments.

When I came out, Waldino smiled at me and said, "Come to my house. There's someone there who wants to see you."

"Who?" I asked.

Johnny waited patiently in Waldino's kitchen. When he saw me, he got up and walked toward me. Waldino acted as our interpreter.

"I'm going to miss you," he said, blushing. "I wanted to give you this at school, but you didn't give me the chance. I hope you like it."

No words in English or Spanish came out of my mouth. Johnny pulled out a gold ring from his jeans' pocket and placed it in the palm of my hand. I held it tight, trembling. I didn't even say thank you. I walked away sweating, thinking, *How in the world am I going to explain this ring to Mamá?*

I went straight to my room to devise a plan. Mamá was outside in the patio hanging clothes to dry. A few minutes later, I knew exactly what to do. I went to the patio and walked past her. While I pretended to smell the freshness of the wet clothes hanging on the clothesline, I tossed the ring on a patch of moist soil that sat against the brick wall. I grabbed some socks to hang and started chatting with Mamá.

"What's for dinner tonight, Mamá?" I asked.

"Chicken soup," she responded.

"Oh, my favorite!" I lied.

A few minutes later, I walked toward the ring and exclaimed, "Look what I found, Mamá!" I made sure I smeared enough mud on the ring so that she would assume it had been buried there for a while.

"Let me see," she said, grabbing it from my hand and looking at me straight in the eye. She cleaned it up and rinsed it with water.

"Let's see if it's real gold," she said, smiling. She brought it to her mouth and sank her teeth in it.

"It's gold!" she assured me. The ring was as thin as the thread she used to sew. It was flexible; it easily bent when I pressed with my two fingers.

Mamá placed the ring on my middle finger and said, "You're so lucky to find such a treasure in our backyard, huh?"

I immediately went back outside the apartments to see if Johnny was still hanging out with Waldino. Waldino was riding his bike while Johnny rode behind him standing, balancing on the back tire rods.

I smiled at them from a distance and lifted my hand to show them the ring on my finger. I enunciated a quiet thank-you with my lips. Johnny understood and smiled. I never saw him again.

District Six

Mamá had always been strict with all three of us throughout our school years. She never allowed us to go on any school field trips near or far. I never bothered to ask her to sign my permission slips during my fourth or fifth grade years at Park Avenue Elementary School. Fifth grade was a blur; all I remember is that I went to school every day and played kickball like a boy. But during sixth grade, I couldn't fool my teacher. She liked me, and she cared for me.

I remember how I couldn't explain to Mrs. Gray that, once again, Mamá hadn't granted me permission to go on the end-of-year school field trip. I was one of the few "blessed" girls in my sixth grade class to have such a strict mother. Mamá didn't allow me to go by myself to the corner bakery to fetch pan dulce, much less go on a field trip that was sixteen miles away.

Her reasons were illogical, according to my classmates and to Mrs. Gray. I can't even recall what bribe she used that morning to convince me to stay home and forget about the infamous field trip to the Griffith Observatory.

The only words I remember coming out of her mouth were "We're in the middle of a war! Who came up with the brilliant idea to go on a field trip during these critical times?" Her lips trembled as she gasped for air to mutter her last word, *críticos*.

The Gulf War didn't allow me to go to Griffith Park. Mamá was petrified; she imagined the worst possible scenarios while my classmates and I rode on the bus. I don't know—maybe she thought a stray bomb would fall from the sky and kill us all.

Mrs. Gray didn't understand why some parents wouldn't allow their children to participate in educational field trips.

Sadly, my English wasn't good enough to give her a detailed explanation. Mrs. Gray tried several times to get it out of me during class, and since I had no words to explain Mamá's way of thinking, she kept me in during recess to try and find out more.

I remember her confused stare, her eyes filled with concern. I was still considered a newcomer from a foreign country, and she needed to expose me to the American world in order to broaden my horizons.

"Why won't your mother let you go on the field trip, Claudia?" she asked.

I detected pain in her voice. My answer was simple and thick with an accent.

"Because of the war," I responded.

With a perplexed look, she questioned me again, "Because of the *what?*"

I replied with a conflicted tone of rage and shame, "Because of the war, Mrs. Gray!"

Of course, my war, the one that my mouth sang that day, did not sound like the war that I spell and pronounce today. It was more like a *whar*: *Becose ouf da whar*.

She continued to question me. I felt desperate. I didn't know how to weave words together in this foreign language. I almost threw myself on the floor to act out a battle scene. Using my own arms, I would pretend to be a soldier shooting at the enemy with a machine gun. The image of me in my mind, crawling on the rug, pretending to be a fallen soldier, was hilarious.

The truth is, I finished growing up in the middle of a silent battlefield in southeast LA. This was a war where the poor lost every day. There was ignorance everywhere. Our enemies were invisible, but they were there. I felt them when I was ten, living in the city of Cudahy.

Ironically, a year before, in 1989, Mamá was forced to accept that I would have to ride on a school bus every day. Park Avenue Elementary became famous from one day to the next.

I saw my neighbors and school friends on Fox News. Some parents were crying, others were enraged. I didn't understand why. Some kids I knew came out on TV stating that they were suffering from headaches, stomachaches, and how they felt nauseous and weak after getting home from school.

Teachers had detected bubbling puddles of oil on my school's playground. I didn't know what to think anymore. I loved my school. I never felt sick with nausea or suffered from headaches. The news lady on channel eleven continued to explain: *"Park Avenue Elementary School was built in 1968 on top of an old landfill, into which industrial wastes had been dumped in the 1930s . . ."*

"No wonder kids feel sick," said Mamá.

"I think I'm starting to feel sick after hearing what they're saying on the news," I said, holding my stomach.

"Oh stop it. Do you really?" Mamá wanted to know.

"No way!" I said, trying to contain my laughter.

Parents and teachers protested in front of the school every day until a few meetings were finally arranged. The school auditorium couldn't hold the multitude of parents who showed up for the meetings. Mamá never liked attending any school meeting. She only met with our teachers for parent conferences.

Our playground was invaded for a couple of weeks by

strangers wearing expensive suits, others wearing orange uniforms with masks and special equipment to dig and test the dirt.

After a few days, my friends and I stopped paying attention to them. We continued to get muddy wallowing in the puddles every day—during recess, during lunch, and after school. Those puddles were fun to splash around in. We didn't know they were toxic. For weeks, we saw the strangers running tests on our playground, but we continued to play, pretending they didn't exist.

District Six eventually took charge of the case. Students were transferred to another school in South-Central Los Angeles, seven miles away. It took the school bus an hour to get us there every morning. Mamá had trouble getting used to this routine. She would drop me off at Park Avenue at seven in the morning, waiting there until I boarded the bus. As soon as I found a seat, she would wave goodbye to me from the window. She would then leave to drop off Consuelo at her middle school, Nimitz.

I rode on that bus for nine months until District Six finally covered the playground surface with a new layer of asphalt—a thicker blacktop. According to some teachers and parents, "They didn't dig deep enough."

A year later, we were back at our school, playing on a greentop. The asphalt was no longer grayish black; District Six had painted it green, a pale green. From afar, it resembled buffalo grass, fine and soft, but we knew all too well that if we stumbled and fell, we would scrape our limbs. I still have the scars.

We Had Our Childhood—Xqab'an cho qaha'lak'uniil

I had already turned thirteen, but still had the mentality of a little girl. I looked, felt, and acted like a ten-year-old. I didn't feel like a teenager; no one saw me like one either, especially not my sisters or Mamá. I didn't get my first period until I was almost sixteen years old.

I loved my two older sisters dearly, but I was obsessed with Consuelo. Whenever I had the chance, I unburied her diary from her bunk-bed mattress. This was the only time I fancied being her age. I secretly wore her shiny bracelets and earrings whenever she wasn't around.

Consuelo was already a señorita at fifteen years old, liking boys and ignoring me more and more every day. I didn't like her snobby friends either. All they cared about was their long, permed hair, and showing off their scrawny legs in pleated miniskirts. I was forever known as Claudia the Tomboy.

Sindy was twenty-one years old going on forty. She thought she'd finally found her way out of Mamá's unrelenting sight by marrying someone twice her age: a paisano, a Guatemalan. He was a grumpy man the same age as Mamá. It was easy for him to steal my sister's heart. Sindy's back had been stamped with Mamá's burning hand too many times, more than Consuelo's or mine. It was the only way Mamá knew how to discipline us, with painful love, as she defined it. People from Mayuelas didn't believe in talking to their children; they believed in belts and shoes and iron whips, whatever object was within their reach.

Mamá's temper escalated every time Sindy snuck out of the house to go on a date with this animal—that's how Mamá referred to him. I didn't want to be in the house when Mamá let it out. Thunder came out of her mouth.

Playing with Cynthia and Lizette, my next-door neighbors, distracted me while Consuelo continued to leave her childhood behind and Sindy forced herself to embrace the early symptoms of menopause, as Mamá would also say. I never understood Sindy. While still living with us at home, she slept all the time. She didn't have friends and didn't socialize much. At the time, I had no idea she was suffering from chronic depression. Mamá didn't understand either, and she beat Sindy constantly, trying to shake some sense into her.

Cynthia and Lizette were two Mexican American siblings, three and two years younger than me. They liked me because I spoke Spanish to them. I didn't understand why they couldn't speak English fluently when they both had been born and raised in the US. I didn't know anything about how the bilingual programs worked because I had been placed in an English-only class upon my arrival from Guatemala. Cynthia and Lisette attended another school where they were placed in a bilingual program. They were mastering their mother tongue so that eventually their English would naturally sink in.

The three of us communicated mainly in Spanish, mixing in English words occasionally. We thought we had created our own language—Mexguatinglish. They spoke "Mexican," and I spoke "Guatemalan."

I lied to them when I told them that I spoke five different languages: Spanish, English, Mexguatinglish, Gerigonza, and Poqomchi'. Gerigonza is like the Spanish version of Pig Latin, where you add the consonants p, f, or t after each vowel of a word's syllable. For example, if I use the letter f, Claudia turns into Clafa-ufu-difi-afa, or if I use the letter *p*, Consuelo turns into Copon-suepe-lopo.

I tried explaining Gerigonza to both Cynthia and Lizette, but the rules were too complex.

Since Gerigonza was too hard for my friends to learn, I decided to teach them a few words in Poqomchi' instead. Poqomchi' is the Mayan language spoken in Tactic. I taught them how to say "little girls" in Poqomchi'. After all, we were k'isa ixq'un playing grown-up games.

Every day we entertained ourselves playing house, tag, hide-and-go-seek, and school, where I was always the k'uh-toom, the teacher at the front of the classroom. And during the hot summers, they always waded in their Intex swimming pool. Mamá didn't want me getting wet in someone else's dirty water. According to Mamá, everyone else's water was always dirty, except ours.

"Mamá," I said one hot afternoon, "Cynthia and Lizette invited me to swim in their pool."

She simply responded, "No!" as she continued to step on the sewing machine pedal. It felt like the engine roared louder than a muscle car while her needle punctuated the fabric at what seemed like a thousand miles an hour. Mamá worked from home as a seamstress. This is how she kept track of every move we made.

"Why not?" I asked.

"Because I said so," she responded, all the while keeping her hand steady and her eyes on the needle.

"Please!" I begged. "It's hot out and they're having fun. I want to swim!"

"No means *no*, Claudia. Don't ask me again!" For a second,

Mamá lifted her head to look me in the face. Her two eyebrows became one dark frown.

"Fine!" I said, rolling my eyes as I stormed off, and left on my bike.

I rode back and forth as I watched Cynthia and Lizette splash each other, trying to get me wet in the process. They looked like little tz'ikins, little birds, bathing in the water. I rode my bike faster and faster around their pool, convincing myself that I was also having fun. I pretended that the water was a green monster trying to chase me.

"What did your mom say, Claudia?" they asked.

"She doesn't want me to get wet cause I'm getting sick," I lied as I continued to circle their pool with my bike. I must have gone around at least fifteen times when I suddenly felt light-headed and fell to the right side, into their pool.

My bike quickly sank, drowning in the water. I immediately pulled it out of the pool and ran back to my house soaked, crying and thinking, *Mamá is going to yank the hair out of my head for getting wet in their "dirty" water.*

When I got home, Mamá immediately stopped her motor and asked, "What the hell happened to you? Why are you crying?" Her steely tone made my teeth chatter even more.

"I . . . I . . . I'm so-sorry! I fell in the pool with the biiiiiiike!" I howled.

Mamá stood quiet for the first time. She stared at me with a smooth forehead. I couldn't detect any bitter lines.

"It was an accident!" I cried.

Mamá's stern face soon cracked with biting laughter. "I wasn't born yesterday! Go get in that filthy water with those girls. Go on, get out of here!"

I couldn't hide my smile as she continued her lecture, "But if you get sick, I will prepare the most revolting purgante you've ever tasted. I don't care if you scream, kick, or faint; I will tie you down and hold your nose until you drink it all." Mamá was capable of doing that and more, all in the name of homemade remedies.

I ran out of the house leaving Mamá's fading words behind. I jumped in the pool wearing my Lycra shorts and a purple shirt. I didn't care that the water was a week old, slimy and green. I was hot, and all I wanted to do was dive underneath the water to cool off and open my eyes to see how the sky looked from underneath the water.

But I couldn't open my eyes. They burned every time I tried. With my eyes shut, I continued to swim, holding my breath like a heavy submarine made out of skin. In the distance I could hear Cynthia and Lisette giggling and proudly speaking Mexiguatinglish.

Middle School

When I finished six grade, I left Park Avenue Elementary behind. I was now in the seventh grade, lost in the elongated dark buildings of my new school—Nimitz Middle School. I was scared. I didn't know anyone. The school was located in the city of Maywood, thirty minutes away from my house. Mamá would drop me off a block away from the main entrance because the traffic in the mornings was unbearable.

On my first day, I walked that entire block to the main gate by myself, feeling empty and ugly, my bowlegs trembling. I felt lonely, like a kid who still belonged in elementary school. Consuelo was a freshman at Bell High School. Mamá would drop me off first and then take Consuelo to the city of Bell.

Consuelo usually waved goodbye from the inside of the car while I secretly wished we were twins so that we could arrive at school together. Sindy was no longer at home. She had moved in with the paisano, the older man who'd stolen her heart. She began attending night school to learn English. I hardly ever saw her.

Nimitz Middle School had a track system because it was so overcrowded. It had four tracks: A, B, C, and D. All my elementary school friends were placed on B track, while I was placed on C track to be on the same track with Consuelo at Bell High School. We were both in school while my friends on B track were on vacation for six weeks. I was miserable without my friends. I felt like I was in jail Monday through Friday from 7:19 a.m. to 3:15 p.m.

I didn't know how I was going to survive my first week of middle school with my limited English. How was I going to deal with seven new teachers? I wasn't placed in ESL classes like Consuelo had been during seventh and eighth grade. *How did she survive Nimitz?* I wondered. *How did she get used to so many different teachers?* I missed Mrs. Gray, my sixth grade teacher.

I had fooled my elementary school teachers into thinking that I was a bright student who had learned how to read and write English even though I had no comprehension of it whatsoever. I had only been in the country for two years. I had even been labeled gifted in the arts by Mrs. Gray. I'd fooled her. I'd fooled my family and friends, everyone, including myself. And now, there I was at a brand-new school where kids were cruel.

In the hallways, I encountered girls who wore lots of makeup. Their lips were smeared with ruby-red lipstick outlined by a purplish lip-liner. Their attitude was bigger than their permed hair, feathered to the side and arched on top with gel or Aqua Net hairspray.

Mamá called them cholitas. Boys who wore baggy pants and had their hair buzzed very short were the cholitos. Everyone was either a cholito or a cholita according to Mamá, whether or not they had short hair or a feathered hairstyle. I stayed away from those girls because they were bossy and brutal.

"To build a tough reputation, they usually shove the quiet girls into the bathroom stalls the first week of school," Consuelo said to me, trying to scare the hell out of me the night before.

"I'm not quiet," I responded, pretending to be brave.

But on my first day of school, I was determined to never go to the bathroom. I didn't even know how to curl my eyelashes at that age. There were no signs of me getting my period any time soon. Some of the girls I saw in the halls looked like they were ready to party at a nightclub. I was terrified to make eye contact with them. I still wore pink shorts and T-shirts. I was thinner than a toothpick and my chest was concave like the underside of a surfboard. Even though I was a seventh grader, I was shorter than most sixth graders. I had to start all over, make new friends and charm the teachers. In every class I sat in the back, unless the teacher had a seating chart.

That first day of school was a nightmare. I got lost several times in the hallways searching for my classes. I couldn't find my assigned locker until the end of the day. When I finally found it, I couldn't figure out how to open it. I had no choice but to carry three heavy books in my backpack and a thick binder in my hands. I was embarrassed to ask anyone for help. I was nervous to put together one complete sentence in English. The school was composed of 99 percent Latinos, yet most pretended not to speak Spanish. I felt lonelier than ever.

During nutrition and lunch everyone seemed to know each other. Some formed their cliques depending on their fashion sense, their manner of speaking or thinking, or their school clubs. I wanted to run and hide in the bathroom, but I was scared of the nasty girls who pretended to own the bathroom and its mirrors. I didn't fit in anywhere. I wasn't a goth chick, a cholita, a cheerleader, a schoolgirl, a nerd, or a jockette. I was a "normal" seventh grader who wore pleated, pink shorts on the first day of school.

As soon as the bell rang for nutrition, I ran to the bathroom before anyone else. My plan was to get there before the cruel girls. I wanted to hide in one of the stalls until the twenty minutes of nutrition were over. I ran to the bathroom down the hall in such a hurry that I didn't notice the girl who was also rushing toward the bathroom door. We crashed into each other trying to enter the bathroom at the same time.

"I'm sorry," she said, trying to gather her things from the floor.

"I'm sorry," I repeated her words as I picked my binder up off the floor.

She had a warm smile on her face. I smiled back at her. Somehow, our loneliness had found each other in the bathroom.

"What's your name?" she asked.

"I'm Claudia," I responded, not knowing whether to shake her hand.

"I'm Annette," she said, as she smiled her lovely smile again. "Are you in any of my classes?"

We compared our schedules and noticed that we had PE together for fourth period. We didn't even bother to use the bathroom. We casually walked out into the hallway together as if we had known each other forever.

I was happy to see her during fourth period. We sat together listening to Ms. Maddy's PE classroom rules and expectations. We were both scared of her. Everyone was terrified of Ms. Maddy—she was loud and tough. I had witnessed her loudness but not her toughness yet. I was relieved when she allowed the students to pick their PE locker partner. Annette and I smiled at each other. We knew we would share PE lockers without having to say a word.

Lunch was right after PE. Annette and I ate together, exchanged phone numbers, and talked about boys. She even tried to help me open my locker, but she failed.

"My locker is in the main building. Why don't you put your books there too?" she offered.

I was too happy to respond. My smile said it all. That day Annette became my best friend. We spent time together during lunch, nutrition, and PE, and the weeks always flew by at school. We had fun talking about girly things, and I felt comfortable being around her because she spoke to me in Spanish without making me feel dumb.

Middle school wasn't so bad after all, thanks to Annette. Sadly, she never came over to my house because of the distance; she lived closer to Nimitz, about twenty-five minutes away from my house. She was also terrified of Mamá. I only got to visit her once, and I ended up getting in trouble for it. Mamá never allowed Consuelo and me to sleep over at our friends' house, and she wouldn't allow us to have any sleepovers at ours either.

Ardor de cuerpo

Reanudar
mis movimientos
repetitivos—

arrancar hojas,
deshojar pieles,
ahogar la mente.

La sensibilidad
se empaña con cada
retuerzo.

La vista pellizcada
se fastidia de tanto ver,
de no ver nada.

La espina quebrantada,
desdoblada se estira
lentamente.

Repetir, repetir,
sin pensar.

Rodillas
que tiemblan—

se doblan repitiendo
el rechinante grito
del hueso ardiente.

Ardor of the Body

To resume
my repetitive
movements—

tear away leaves,
unpeel layers,
drown the mind.

The sensibility blurs
with every
twist and turn.

Compressed sight withers
from constant looking,
without seeing anything.

Split, the deteriorating
spine unfolds,
slowly.

Tedious, tedious,
without thinking.

Knees
that tremble—

they fold repeating
the screeching shriek
of the ardent bone.

Lentils, Anyone?

Once in a while, my parents would make "fun" plans for the weekend so that Consuelo and I wouldn't ask for sleepovers or to spend time with our friends outside the house. One particular weekend, Mamá had the brilliant idea to visit Glenda, my stepdad's sister, who lived in the valley about two hours away. I loved visiting Glenda and her family, but that day I wasn't in the mood to visit her or spend four hours trapped in the back of the car with Consuelo.

"I don't feel like going to Glenda's," I said to Mamá when she tried to hurry me. She almost had a heart attack.

"Who do you think you are? Of course you're going!" she said, pressing her pointer finger into my chest.

Her eyes got big and watery as she got closer to my face and said, "You can't stay home alone. You're only thirteen years old. So get ready."

"Well, I'm not going!" I yelled, running to my room and leaping onto my bunk bed. I hid under the covers and immediately began sweating because I knew better than to defy Mamá. I was expecting her to yank the covers off of me or pull me out of bed by my hair, but she didn't. She walked out of my room and muttered something to Amado. I couldn't hear what she said to him.

A few minutes later, everyone was ready. From my room, I heard Mamá locking the door. I couldn't believe she allowed me to stay home alone. She let me be for the first time. It was early morning, and I knew they wouldn't be back until late that night. I had the whole day to myself. I immediately jumped out of bed, and the first thing I did was call Annette.

"Come over to my house," she said.

"Who's going to pick me up?" I asked. "You live too far away."

"Walk over and I'll meet you halfway."

I was ready for an adventure. I showered, got dressed, and snuck out through my bedroom window. Mamá had locked both doors, and I couldn't open them without the key. I carefully removed the window screen, climbed over the window-sill, and jumped out of the house, landing like a cat. I closed the window and placed the window screen back. Breaking into or out of my house was too easy. The realization kind of scared me.

I began my fast-paced journey to Annette's house. I had never walked such a long distance on my own in the US. I didn't make eye contact with anyone driving or anyone who passed me walking on the street. I kept my face glued to the cement. I felt guilty knowing that I was being sneaky. It took me almost forty minutes to get to the 99 Cents Only store where Annette and I planned to meet.

"You made it!" she said. "Wow, you're sweaty."

I wiped my forehead with my shirt's sleeve and said, "I have five dollars. Let's buy candy and ice cream."

Annette had some spare change, too. We got some Corn Nuts, neapolitan ice-cream sandwiches, and two KitKat bars. It took us about twenty-five minutes to get to her house from the store. We were having such a good time walking together that it never occurred to me that it was going to take me more than an hour to walk back home.

The day went by fast hanging out with Annette. We talked about everything, from boys and school to our breasts and periods. Annette had the biggest boobs I had seen on a twelve-year-old. She'd begun menstruating at the age of ten. She was surprised that I still hadn't gotten my period.

"You're so lucky," she said.

"I know," I lied, pretending that I wasn't dying to get mine.

Annette's mom was kind and soft-spoken. She bought us a pizza for dinner, but somehow forgot to ask me when or who was going to pick me up. She didn't drive and her husband wasn't yet home from work.

As it got darker, I began to feel sick to my stomach. I was scared to walk back home alone. I pretended not to care as I continued to comb Annette's hair. She had already teased and sprayed my copete. I was pretending to have fun. I was good at taming my anxiety.

In the middle of our pretend beauty salon, Annette's mother came in the room and handed me the phone.

"It's your mom," she said.

I felt like fainting. *How did she get Annette's number?*

I grabbed the phone and in an unsure, squeaky voice said, "Hello?"

"There you are!" Mamá's voice quivered.

She sounded weak, like she had been crying for days, but then her tone changed. "We have been worried sick about you, and you don't bother to call or leave us a note? We searched all over the neighborhood, and nothing. I almost called the police!"

Her voice continued to gain momentum and power. "Give me Annette's address. I want you to wait for me outside her house. I don't want to see or speak to anyone, do you understand?"

"Yes," I said.

"I'll be there in twenty-five minutes."

I broke down in front of Annette.

"Why are you so scared of your mom, Claudia?" she asked.

"You have no idea what she's capable of," I admitted.

Annette hugged me and walked me outside.

"I need to be alone because I'm not sure what Mamá is planning to do or how she is going to react," I said.

"I understand," said Annette.

I sat on the curb, anxiously waiting for Mamá. I drew stick figures in the dirt with a pebble. I cried just imagining what she would do to me. *Would she hit me with a belt and pull my hair in the middle of the street, Mamatoya style?*

A few minutes later, she pulled up in her gray, four-door Honda Accord. She unlocked the door and gestured me to get in. I got in. She didn't say a word to me. She didn't even bother to look at me. I shivered from the cold and the thought of the physical pain she was planning to inflict on me.

Mamá's eyes were puffy and red. I began to wonder if she felt remorse for leaving me locked up in the house. Or maybe she thought that someone had kidnapped me and she was just grateful to see me alive. The twenty-five minutes on the road were quiet and long. Even her silence took the form of a slow-motion ache.

When we arrived home, before stepping out of the car, with the softest voice she said, "Go inside, put on some shorts, and come to the kitchen."

My jaw almost got stuck in an awkward *O* position. I knew for sure that she was going to whip me, but I wondered with what.

I walked inside the house quietly crying, my face defeated. Amado was sitting in the dining room looking down. Instead of looking upset or concerned, he looked sad as if somebody had died. I went straight to my room. Consuelo was sitting on her bed looking mad.

"You're so stupid, Claudia!" She shook her head in disappointment and continued, "I was forced to give out Annette's number. We were worried about you!"

I had nothing to say. I continued to cry quietly as I got undressed. I was terrified to walk out to the living room, to the kitchen, where Mamá was waiting for me. *What was she planning?*

Amado tried to dissuade her.

"Talk to her instead," I heard him say.

"Don't tell me how to discipline my daughter!" Mamá snapped.

Amado walked off and shut himself in their bedroom. I was standing in the middle of the living room pretending to be tough. No more signs of tears were on my face.

"Come here," Mamá demanded.

I walked over to the kitchen. I hadn't noticed the pile of lentils she had spread on the floor. I was confused. I wasn't sure what she expected me to do with the lentils. *Eat them raw? Sort them out or pick them up, one by one with my tongue?*

Then she said, "Kneel here!" She pointed to the lentils. I thought it was a joke. I wanted to laugh, but I knew better. Then I thought, *This is going to be a piece of cake. I can pretend that this is painful, the worst punishment ever. I can fool everyone and become an easy martyr.*

I knelt on the lentils wearing my old pajama shorts.

"Don't get up until I say so," she commanded.

I didn't respond. I did as she told me. I sat back and rested my butt on my calves.

"Sit up, kneel high!" she said.

I couldn't help but smirk, and she noticed my small act of defiance. I did exactly what she wanted me to do. I knelt high. I pretended to be praying. Laughing at Mamá's idea of punishment inside my head. I kept thinking how I was going to play it off and make it seem that this was the worst thing she had ever done to me. But five minutes in, the lentils started to cut into the skin on my knees. Fifteen minutes into it, my legs were numb. I couldn't move.

That's when it hit me. *This woman knows what she's doing. I'll show her how tough I am. I can kneel for hours if I have to. I can prove my point.*

An hour passed, and I could feel each lentil seed perforating my skin, one by one. I couldn't tell just by looking at it because I couldn't move, but I was sure they had become part of me. Tears of rage and pain began rolling down my cheeks. Mamá sat on a chair across from me, staring at me, her silent glare telling me that she had won the battle and to never defy her again.

I closed my eyes but the tears inevitably kept coming. Amado stepped out of the bedroom and went to get a glass of water.

"That's enough, Victoria," he said, again trying to defend me.

"Not yet," she said.

"I can stay here all night long!" I yelled back, hiding my tears behind my palms. Soon my sobs turned into a burst of bitter laughter. Crying, laughing, crying, laughing, like a mad child—a wounded animal.

Mamá let another hour go by. My laughter must have stabbed her deep inside. Thank goodness I didn't feel the pain anymore. My knees were locked. I was bleeding from the small cuts the lentil seeds had produced. I kept crying with anger. I'm pretty sure Mamá recognized that anger well. It was the only type of tears she would exhibit in front of us.

Amado came out of his room another time. He began arguing with Mamá.

"Get her off the floor, now!" he insisted.

"Let her get up on her own," she responded.

I tried to get up but I couldn't. The bottom half of my body felt dead. I began to shout, "I can't get up. I can't!"

Amado began to cry. He tried to pick me up from behind, by my arms, but I refused. I wanted to get up on my own and walk to my room. I wanted to show Mamá that she had not defeated me, but I couldn't move at all. I began to cry inconsolably, again.

Amado ended up picking me up and carrying me to my room. I lay on the top bunk, shocked, letting what Mamá had done to me sink in. Consuelo didn't say a word. I heard her sobbing through the night.

It's Been A While Since I Heard Your Last Song

Ya no cantes tu canto desde tu jaula, Cenzontle. ¡Libérate!

Do not sing from a cage—

Bellow your 400 poems from the distance of your silenced home:
Yes, mockingbird, your feathers have bones. Eres pájaro, vuela.

Reinvent your wings. Spread them out, you are not
a flightless bird. Never sing the song
of another caged bird.

Cenzontle,

Forget the branch of the weeping willow. Venture out to
palos verdes and sugar pines.
But build your nest here, on the branches of my ceiba tree.

Ya no cantes tu canto desde tu jaula, Cenzontle. ¡Libérate!
Do not sing from a cage.

PART IV

RETURNING TO MY MOTHERLAND

Kim Ayu—Vení Pa' ca

Mis entrañas se contraen
Es mi aliento que se escapa
Va en busca de mi gente

Oigo un eco que retumba
Voces dulces, lengua tierna:

Kim ayu—vení pa' ca

Corre viento que me roza
Con olor a incienso
La marimba se oye lejos

Son los moros, han llegado
Con sus danzas de venados

Oigo un eco que retumba
Voces dulces, lengua tierna:

Kim ayu—vení pa' ca

Los repiques de campanas en
Los templos siempre estallan
Ese acorde no se olvida

En mi piel cae la cera
Esta quema, y hace llagas

Que me adiestran a apreciar
Mi nueva existencia

Oigo un eco que retumba
Voces dulces, lengua tierna:

Kim ayu—vení pa' ca

Mi alma ruge, ya no tiembla,
Ha encontrado al nuevo Edén.

(En Poqomchi') "Suk Nuk'uxl—
Mi corazón está contento."

Kim Ayu—Come Over Here

My insides contract
It is my breath that escapes
It goes in search of my people

I hear an echo that resonates
Sweet voices, tender tongue:

Kim ayu—come over here

A wind of incense grazes my core
The marimba's keys
Chime in the distance

It is the moors, they have come
With their ancient deer dances

I hear an echo that resonates
Sweet voices, tender tongue:

Kim ayu—come over here

The clamor of the bells
From the temple resound
That melody can never fade

On my flesh I feel a wax burning
It leaves scars that teach me
To appreciate my new existence

I hear an echo that resonates
Sweet voices, tender tongue:

Kim ayu—come over here

My fierce soul no longer trembles
I have found my new Edén.

(En Poqomchi') "Suk Nuk'uxl—
My heart is content."

The Return

"Your mother never shed a tear out of self-pity. Those tears were not of anguish, or fear. They were cries of anger. Tears of hunger." Tía Soila's voice was shaking as she said this to Consuelo. Consuelo was listening attentively.

We were back in Mayuelas. We were back in our humid village where the mango and the tamarindo trees were the only things that kept Tía Soila's house fresh under a blanket of shade. It was 1992, and we were back in Guatemala after living in the US for three years. I was thirteen years old and Consuelo fifteen. Mamá, Consuelo, and I were back to file our papers through the Amnesty Program. Sindy couldn't return with us because she was on the verge of giving birth to her first son, my nephew, Andrew.

Mamá explained how Sindy couldn't be added to the Amnesty Program because she was already over twenty-one and practically married. Sindy had moved out of the house, and I was crushed knowing that she couldn't come with us. She gave birth alone in the US. No one was there to kiss her and bring her flowers. She was alone with the father of her son. Her depression became chronic.

I was still in disbelief that we were in the process of becoming residents of the US. Nobody was going to call me an illegal alien ever again. César, my former fifth grade classmate, would have to take all his insults back.

I was thrilled to be back. Everyone clapped when the plane landed. Some people cried tears of happiness. Others simply hugged each other. I hugged Consuelo because she was sitting next to me. Mamá sat across the aisle from us. I noticed a tear rolling down her cheek.

Three years had passed yet Tía Soila's house looked the same. The dirt-floor patio was still filled with mango and tamarindo trees. Her kitchen still had an adobe wall adjacent to the bedroom wall. A rainbow hammock still hung in the middle of the corridor waiting for one of us to lie on it. And Tía Soila had not aged. She looked the same, dark and thin. Her voice had changed though; it had become hoarse. It felt great to see her. She was the only one out of the whole family who never expected anything from us. Not even a pack of gum.

She wasn't as tall as I remembered. When I saw her, I dropped my two bags and ran to her. We held each other for a couple of seconds. She still smelled like a mixture of cigarette smoke and grapefruit rind, which clung to her skin, clothes, and silver hair. Both Consuelo and Mamá hugged her at the same time. She was speechless. Tears gently rolled down her wrinkly, tanned cheeks. Everyone cried, except for me. I was overwhelmed with excitement.

Tía Soila had the biggest, most beautiful smile. She had finally gotten used to her dentures.

"Her gums learned to harden, just like her lifestyle," said Mamá.

"How long did it take you to get used to your new teeth?" I wanted to know.

"A long time. I didn't wear them for a couple of years because they hurt my gums," she admitted.

"Her gums are hard now and so are her hands," added Mamá.

Sitting there, watching her interact with Mamá and Consuelo, reminded me of all the things we did together before immigrating to the US. Tía Soila would take me to el monte, the woods, to chop off the branches of ceiba trees with her machete. She fastened the leña, the firewood, with a rope and placed it on her head. Her yagual, a folded bandana, served as a cushion between her crown and the heaviness of the bundle.

She balanced the firewood on her head just like she did with the cántaro full of water, just like she did with the broken palangana full of people's dirty clothes, just like she did while pretending to tame her hunger for solitude.

The river, el monte, her cracked adobe kitchen walls, su delantal—her apron—and the heat of her comal and iron will perpetually live within me.

Tía Soila has always been a breathing poem who knows how to climb the tallest tamarindo trees. She's one of those epic women who makes people smile when she passes by, flaunting her thin thighs, her breast—unbroken. She wears no bra. She walks the streets of Mayuelas, selling her numbers with an impeccable posture.

Mamá hugged her again. They didn't let go of each other for some time. Trying to hide her tears, Mamá told her, "Tía Soila, I brought you some hair dye to hide your white canas."

They both exploded with laughter as they sat on the wooden bench leaning against the kitchen's adobe wall. It was time to reminisce about the past. We left our bags in the middle of the corridor. I knew exactly what story they were going to recall. I sat still, silent with expectation. Crossing my fingers, I hoped they might reveal something new about Mamá's past.

"Your mother is a silent warrior who never tells her stories," said Tía Soila. "She has always been too proud to show people her scars."

I had always wanted to know all of Mamá's secrets. Mamá was bitter about life and I wanted to know why: Why she stopped smiling one day. Why the short hair. She taught my sisters and I to never get close to family. Her advice was always the same: "Don't look for family! Family members only look for you when they need something from you—only to screw you over and over; it's just you three, always help each other. You and your sisters should always stick together and help each other so that you don't depend on others."

But Tía Soila was the exception. She was everything to Mamá.

Va callada

absorbiendo el silencio
de senderos polvorientos,

atestados de flores muertas
de la sed: Madrecacao,

Malvas, Petunias, a veces hasta los
Pensamientos se secan y se queman.

Aligerada huye de la sombra
alargada de una mujer desdeñada:

va en busca de agua fresca . . .

con su yagual enrollado en la cabeza
balancea un cántaro quebrantado—

ya no zarandea sus caderas
redondas, ceñidas—

hunde ambas manos en los huecos
profundos de su delantal.

A lo lejos oye el río;
se oye bravo.

Quietly, she goes,

absorbing the silence
of dusty paths,

saturated with wild flowers
dying of thirst: Madrecacao,

Malvas, Petunias, sometimes
even Pensamientos, dry and burn.

Hurriedly, she flees
from the elongated shade

of a forgotten woman:
she goes in search of fresh,

new water . . .

with her yagual
wrapped around her head,

she balances a broken cántaro—

she no longer sways her dented/
rounded hips—

she sinks both hands
into the hollows of her apron.

Far away,
she hears the deafening river.

Victoria

Tía Soila took out a pack of menthol cigarettes. She hit the end three times with her bare palm to break them loose; I sat there in silence contemplating her ritual. She lit one cigarette and inhaled. Her dimples seemed to connect inside her mouth. Then she slowly exhaled the smoke through her nose like one of those mobsters who was getting ready to talk serious business, just like I had seen in *The Godfather*.

After taking a couple of drags, Tía Soila began Mamá's story.

"At the age of eight, your mother ruled the streets of Mayuelas. She was a chunky little tomboy with a braid on each side of her head. She was afraid of the toma, the thing that terrified her the most when it got dark. She played from dawn to dusk until she would holler for me, *Tía Soila, come get me, please!* I'd help her cross the dark side of the toma that was under the shade of the biggest mango tree from the house. This mango tree, she said, had the shape of a witch's face. Always sweating, running from here to there, tishuda—barefoot. Her thick lips popping out because of her crooked top front teeth. She listened to no one, and no one dare messed with her on the streets. She had a reputation of beating up kids who bothered her about her looks and teeth. This made her strong—invincible.

"Victoria, do you remember the day I found out you were pregnant? I held you in my arms cussing you out at the same time. You were so stupid and young."

Mamá agreed and couldn't help but hide a smile full of shame. Tía Soila's eyes were on us now. She continued, "Your mother got pregnant at a very young age." I already knew that.

At the age of fifteen she had given birth to a dead child. She never bothered to name her. I was afraid to ask why.

Tía Soila stopped again and from her corridor bench where we were all sitting, she gazed at the distant burning sky with a blank stare. She took another drag of her menthol cigarette. Mamá stayed quiet. We all did. Tía Soila's opening line was going exactly where I wanted it to go: Mamá's youth.

Sindy was born when Mamá was only seventeen. Consuelo was born six years later, and I was born two years after Consuelo. Mamá was a twenty-five-year-old woman with a second grade education raising three daughters, most of the time alone; I vaguely remember Papá being around. And when he was in the picture, he was usually drunk and fighting with Mamá.

"When your mother was little," Tía Soila continued, "she went through many phases in her life. She was young and didn't know how to raise a baby girl all by herself without a partner. She had barely finished raising herself on the streets, selling mangoes and grapefruit or whatever fruit she got from the trees she rocked."

A mocking laugh shook her thin body. "We have all gone through the same hell," Tía Soila added nonchalantly.

Mamatoya remarried when Mamá was six years old. She left her old life behind, including Mamá, to move to Tactic.

"I'll look after her. She won't go hungry with me," said Tía Soila to Mamatoya as she boarded the guagua headed to El Rancho, the midpoint between Mayuelas and Tactic.

"Tía Soila was my hero. I knew I could always count on her," cut in Mamá, finally boasting about her childhood adventures. "What I really enjoyed doing at the age of eight, nine, and ten was cleaning Alba's diner. I'd wash dishes, wipe down the tables, and eat for free. And if I wanted to buy a dress, or a pair of new shoes, I climbed the mango and grapefruit trees to fetch the fruit and sell it to the people boarding the guaguas," Mamá said.

Mamá always reminded us how much she resented Mamatoya, her mother, for choosing Don Lalo over her. She admitted enjoying her childhood freedom, though. Tía Soila was like an older sister who couldn't control her, but she was there to console her whenever she made mistakes or someone broke her heart.

I never quite understood how she enjoyed that freedom. I know I wouldn't have at her age. I always wanted Mamá around. I had missed her terribly the three years she was gone. But she had had no choice. Mamá immigrated to the US in search of a better life for herself, for us, and to run away from Papá, whose toxic love was destroying her.

"Those were the days when your mother barely had enough to feed herself. But Sindy found the perfect way to deal with her hunger," said Tía Soila.

"Sindy waited patiently for your mother to finish washing Doña Petronila's dirty clothes. The pila withered your mother's hands every day. Every night she rubbed them with lotion. Tears erupted from her eyes when she counted the few quetzales that she earned at the end of the month."

At the age of twenty-one, she didn't know how to discipline Sindy. Sindy was only four years old, and she loved to eat mud like it was chocolate pudding.

Tía Soila continued, "Your mother would sit Sindy down on top of the wobbly wooden dinner table that was next to the pila. The pila was against one of the walls that connected the kitchen with the outdoor dining patio. Poor Sindy had a fear of heights. She didn't dare move. And your mother knew this well."

"But Sindy was clever enough to balance herself on the center of the table by leaning against one of the walls," added Mamá.

Consuelo and I laughed picturing Sindy sitting on the table, terrified of heights.

"She sat there quietly, patiently, observing how Victoria slammed her hips against the pila trying to beat each dirty garment with her bare fists. She had already broken the other side of the washbasin," said Tía Soila.

Tía Soila pointed to the far-left corner of the garden. We all turned, and under the shade of the biggest grapefruit tree, we saw Mamá's broken pila buried halfway into the ground. The right side was still broken, but the left side had lavender bellflowers blooming. Its light green vine had wrapped itself on the broken side of the washbasin.

"Your mother was famous for being one of the most reliable lavanderas in town," Tía Soila boasted. "She washed people's clothes better than her own. She was also famous for stealing detergent from Gualán's mercado, and hiding it well in her soaked apron.

"The outline of the bar of soap was obvious in her apron's pocket, but nobody ever dared accuse your mother of stealing anything. Her apron was never dry. Always wet, always," chuckled Tía Soila.

Suddenly I heard Mamá mumbling between her lips, "Filthy people! But Sindy and I ate with those nickels and dimes."

"Sindy eventually learned to cope with her phobia," Tía Soila continued. "While sitting on the wobbly table, she found her haven. Her favorite wall—made out of clay, mud, and hay—nurtured her while she waited long hours for your mother to wash and hang people's clothes to dry.

"Your mother's chores seemed to go on forever, but Sindy never complained. She was happy to be placed next to her muddy wall. After gathering the dry clothes in her broken bowl, your mother was ready to attack a pile of clean, dried clothes that needed to be press-ironed. Your mother had an established routine, and she knew better than to leave the ironing until the end of the day."

Mamá interrupted Tía Soila, "I didn't want my hands to curl up with rheumatism for wetting them after absorbing the heat of the iron. I was tired of being burned by life."

Tía Soila nodded. She knew well the life of a lavandera. She was still washing people's dirty clothes even though both her sons lived in the US, and sometimes forgot to send her money.

Tía Soila continued, "To keep an eye on your sister, your mother would set her ironing board on the kitchen table right next to her. She folded three to four towels over the table so the heat of the iron wouldn't penetrate the wood. This was your mother's routine every other day."

Mamá sat quietly, nodding her head.

"The comal was fueled with burning coals throughout the day. Carefully, she picked up the blazing coals with a spatula and placed them in the rusted pressing iron. Her iron weighed more than your skinny sister. Even though she was skin and bones, Sindy's belly was bigger than her head. Your mother constantly mocked her bubble belly by saying, *The tapeworms are eating you alive from all the mud you gobble up.* Your sister knew to stay quiet."

Tía Soila paused to light another cigarette and then went on.

"Sindy carefully watched your mother's movements. She was afraid to move. On one side, there was heat and on the other side, there was height. Either way, she was damned.

"Your sister was always hungry, but not for love. She was not hungry for food, either. She simply loved the way her teeth crushed the clumps of mud in her mouth. She craved mud more than anything else.

"One day, she leaned her head against the wall and discovered a hole. It was a tiny muddy hole. Discretely, she hid both hands behind her back, and with one of her little fingers began making the hole in the wall bigger. She felt the prickly hay poke one of her fingers. She bled, but she didn't cry because she knew that she had found her paradise—a heaven full of mud.

"Your mother thought she had found the perfect solution to your sister's eating habit by sitting her on the table. A week later, she noticed the big hole in the wall. Your mother scolded her again and again. Sindy never learned.

"A month later, your mother and I found more holes. I became obsessed with the idea that somebody had given your sister a mal de ojo, the evil eye, or that she was possessed. I convinced your mother to call the town's curandera to come and do a limpia, a spiritual cleansing, on your sister.

"Doña Tomasa, the town's healer, came and did the cleansing right away. She burned incense, lit some candles, and whipped the walls with ruda, long sprigs of rue. Doña Tomasa passed the rue over Sindy's body. The smell made your sister gag. She couldn't stand the smell of it and vomited up all the mud in her stomach.

"Finally, Doña Tomasa rubbed an egg on Sindy's head. She closed her eyes and spoke in tongues. To finish the ritual, she broke the egg and emptied it into a glass of water. The egg came out fully transparent. There were no threads or bubbles. We knew then your sister had been cured of the evil eye.

"After the Santería ritual, your sister stayed away from the walls inside the house, but she couldn't resist the outdoor walls. Those were also rich with clay and mud. The temptation was too much for her.

"One day, your mother caught her little fingers digging a hole in the patio wall. Your mother couldn't help laughing, but in the midst of her laughter, she broke out into sobs that made her tremble. Your mother was hungry. And so was your sister."

"We were all hungry," interrupted a high-pitched voice from the kitchen. It was Mamatoya, accompanied by Tía Negra. I couldn't believe my eyes. My abuelita was in our presence; I had missed her patchouli smell these last three years. Her short, black, curly hair—still the same. Her freckles spread over her face like tiny wild-flower seeds. Her thin lips, pink and soft, but firm. La mera mera, Mamatoya, was now in the middle of our conversation. Consuelo and I ran up to them. I hugged la Negra first, and then timidly hugged Mamatoya. La Negra was there with her beautiful energy—soft spoken and gentle. She attracted not just the mosquitoes, but all of us, especially Mamá, who felt comfortable around her, opening up like a pink cactus flower.

I was thrilled to see them. I noticed how Mamá got

teary-eyed and was the last one to embrace Mamatoya, but she did, nonetheless. I was proud of her. The six of us sat there in silence for a while. It was somewhat awkward, until Tía Soila said, "Weren't we all hungry?"

Mamá couldn't hold it in any longer and burst into tears, her heart broken. She had been holding back for her entire life, since she was six years old, and she finally let it out in front of all of us. I didn't know what to say or do. None us did. La Negra finally put her hand on Mamá's back to comfort her.

I remembered how Mamatoya always said that Mamá didn't want to live with her in Tactic after she married Don Lalo. That had never made any sense to me. I always wondered why Mamá would've wanted to leave her mother's side at such a young age. That was Mamatoya's story, but Mamá said that Mamatoya left her behind. And I believed Mamá.

Mamatoya always had a story to tell at every gathering. And this was no exception. I watched her wring her hands nervously and bite her bottom lip. Her eyes seemed to glaze over while her voice became clear and sharp from her gut.

"I have suffered all my life," she began. "Since I was a child. When I was only twelve years old, I was the oldest of five siblings and practically in charge of the household when Mamita gave birth to twins."

Mamita was my great-grandmother. Mamatoya sat down on a stool and rubbed her knees together. She sighed heavily and continued her story.

"She named the boys Hector and Agusto. Everyone in the house loved the twins. They were a rarity, a blessing. Soila was nine, three years younger than me. Mamita gave Hector to

Soila and Agusto to me to take care of. It was customary back then to make your older children take care of the younger children."

Mamatoya stopped and looked up at a hole in the sheet-metal ceiling, avoiding eye contact with Mamá. We all sat there in silence, waiting for her to go on.

"I remember when Mamita gave Agusto to me. She said, *You're in charge of him. Don't drop him!* I was to change his pañal and bring him to Mamita every time he needed to be breastfed. I was his babysitter during the day. Mamita would wrap him on my back with a shawl, and I would carry him everywhere I went, whether it be to the store or the river to wash clothes— he went everywhere with me. I loved my little brother."

"And I loved Hector," said Tía Soila.

Mamatoya took out her handkerchief from her bra to wipe away her tears. "It was as if we both had live dolls to play with. We took good care of our little brothers. We played with them. We changed their dirty clothes. We made sure they got fed on time, every day." She paused, then cried out, "But it wasn't my fault, it wasn't my fault!"

"No one is blaming you, Toya," said Tía Soila.

Mamatoya continued wringing her hands and cracking her knuckles as she spoke.

"Months went by, and at first the twins grew strong and healthy. But suddenly Agusto became ill with Typhoid fever, and I couldn't do anything to make him better. I tried all types of remedies on him, but nothing worked. By the time Mamita realized what was happening, it was too late. The only doctor in the village couldn't do anything, either. Agusto passed away two days later. I never forgave myself."

Mamatoya began to sob. I got up and I hugged her. Within a few minutes, she wiped her tears and cleared her throat.

"Hector lived, and he and Soila became close as they grew older. As I aged, I continued to blame myself for my brother's death. I felt like I could never take care of another human being. When you were born, Victoria, I was only seventeen, still a child. And when I moved to Tactic with Lalo, I couldn't make you come live with me. How could I? In my mind, I had killed an innocent child. Who was I to force you?"

Mamatoya slowly rose from her stool and approached Mamá, taking her hand. Surprisingly, Mamá didn't pull away. Mamatoya pleaded for forgiveness in front of all of us.

"I love you," she said. "I'm so sorry for hurting you, for abandoning you. But I couldn't force you to live with Lalo and me. I had a tough life. I know it's no excuse. If I could do things differently, I would. I regret it every day of my life, believe me. Please forgive me."

We all sat there crying together. I'm not sure if Mamá forgave Mamatoya. She never responded, only sat there weeping.

As We Go

A ti, Madre

Today,
I come back to see the years in your face—deep
lines that spread with your Mona-Victoria smile.

And you know so well what I seek in you—

I am here to rest my languid body on your petate of hay,
I am not searching for pity; I am hungry for faith.
My body has shattered my soul into rain.

And I know so well what I seek in you—

I don't want to drink your words; I come to immerse myself
in the river that let me go. Unstitch my hidden veins,
Madre, unstitch them before I drown.

EPILOGUE

¿Quién soy yo para juzgar? Never have I kneaded the masa in either Mamá's or Mamatoya's metate. But I am happy to have been ground so fine in their metate just like the resilient black corn that takes time to cook on the comal.

When Mamá first left for El Norte, every grown-up told me that it was a matter of life and death. But what did that matter to my seven-year-old mind? When I woke up to find Mamá gone, I was devastated, my heart shattered into pieces. I wondered if a corner of my heart resented Mamá for abandoning me for three years, just like Mamatoya abandoned her when she was six.

But Mamá was able to stich my heart back together when she returned for us. I now understand how Mamá's trip to El Norte was ultimately a journey of sacrifice, a sacrifice for us. My heart doesn't ache anymore. I can only hope that Mamatoya was able to mend Mamá's heart with her apology, and that her heart isn't broken anymore.

I am thankful to have been raised by this pack of matriarchs—a pack of she-wolves. I am the sompopo, I am the diablita, I am the abispa I am today because of Mamatoya, Tía Soila, and Mamá. Women who passed down their hunger for love and forgiveness. These women will always be the tusas, the husk to my corn.

ACKNOWLEDGMENTS

I would like to acknowledge the generous assistance of my mentors at Antioch: Kerry Madden, Gayle Brandeis, Carol Potter, and Todd Mitchell for helping me complete this memoir. I would also like to thank Dr. Matthew Becker for reading my manuscript and offering valuable suggestions. Thank you, Robyn Hernández, for proofreading it; I loved your close reading.

Thank you to the Feminist Press for supporting the work of women and nonbinary writers of color and also for creating the Louise Meriwether First Book Prize. It's truly an honor to be the 2018 recipient.

Thank you to my Escritores: Pluma y Corazón who helped me focus with my poetry and short stories. Yes, that's you, Robyn, Carlos, Marcos, and my beautiful Nacor. Thank you for meeting once a month, reading my pieces, and giving me precious feedback.

Furthermore, I would like to thank Victor for his support, encouragement, and gentle patience while we were still married when I began writing some of these poems and essays.

I cannot forget to thank my family in Guatemala for being unique and full of hunger, especially my mother's visceral courage. Thank you, Mami, for being so courageous and for sacrificing your life twice for us when crossing the border. You are a true inspiration. Gracias, Amado, for loving all of us.

Thank you, Mamatoya and Tía Soila, for simply being yourselves: grand and exquisite. Thank you for your childhood stories that completed my story.

Warmest gratitude to my editor at the Feminist Press, Lauren Rosemary Hook, who's brilliant and pure magic when it comes to editing.

Thank you, Josie Mendez-Negrete, for always believing in me. For always having words of encouragement and beauty when it comes to my writing and art.

Immense gratitude to my partner, Nacor, my love, who allows me to be. Thank you for your delicious meals, for nourishing me, for reminding me when to take my meds, for proofreading my work, for your patience, and for understanding this crazy heart of mine.

A heartfelt thank you to my sisters, Consuelo and Sindy, whom I respect and love con todo corazón. Thank you for allowing me to write about our life, our stories.

Finally, and most importantly, I would like to thank my daughter, Alexa, for her quietness and tolerance.

PREVIOUSLY PUBLISHED WORK

I would like to thank the editors of the following online journals, literary journals, and anthologies, in which poems and essays in this book first appeared:

nineteen sixty nine: an ethnic studies journal

Chicana / Latina Studies: The Journal of Mujeres Activas en Letras y Cambio Social

Nobantu Project

La Noria Literary Journal

Texas Poetry Calendar

Mom Egg Review

Berkeley Poetry Review

Poetry of Resistance: A Multicultural Anthology in Response to Arizona SB 1070, Xenophobia and Injustice

Apiary

La Tolteca

Somos en escrito: The Latino Literary Magazine

Southern Humanities Review

wildness

The Wandering Song: Central American Writing in the United States

San Diego Reader

Fifth Wednesday Journal

More Narrative Nonfiction from the Feminist Press

Against Memoir: Complaints, Confessions & Criticisms
by Michelle Tea

Among the White Moon Faces:
An Asian-American Memoir of Homelands
by Shirley Geok-lin Lim

Black Dove: Mamá, Mi'jo, and Me
by Ana Castillo

Born in the Big Rains:
A Memoir of Somalia and Survival
by Fadumo Korn

Dreaming of Baghdad by Haifa Zangana

Spit and Passion by Cristy C. Road

Tenemental: Adventures of a Reluctant Landlady
by Vikki Warner

Testo Junkie: Sex, Drugs, and Biopolitics
in the Pharmacopornographic Era
by Paul B. Preciado

Translation as Transhumance by Mireille Gansel

The War Before: The True Life Story of
Becoming a Black Panther, Keeping the Faith in Prison
& Fighting for Those Left Behind
by Safiya Bukhari